Digital Photo Editing with Picasa for Seniors

Studio Visual Steps

Digital Photo Editing with Picasa for Seniors

Get Acquainted with Picasa: Free, Easy-to-Use Photo Editing Software

Visual Steps™
www.visualsteps.com

This book has been written using the Visual Steps™ method.
Cover design by Studio Willemien Haagsma bNO

© 2014 Visual Steps
Author: Studio Visual Steps

First printing: February 2014
ISBN 978 90 5905 368 7

Resources used: Some of the computer terms and definitions seen here in this book have been taken from descriptions found online at the Windows Help and Support website or the Picasa website.

Do you have questions or suggestions?
E-mail: info@visualsteps.com

Would you like more information?
www.visualsteps.com

Website for this book:
www.visualsteps.com/picasaseniors
Here you can register your book.

Subscribe to the free Visual Steps Newsletter:
www.visualsteps.com/newsletter

Table of Contents

Foreword

Picasa is a very popular and free program for managing and editing digital photos. You can sort and arrange photos into albums and add titles or tags to your photos so they are easier to find. You can choose to have this extra information displayed below the thumbnail images in the *Picasa* library screen.

Picasa also offers a variety of photo editing options. In this book you will learn how to apply automatic and manual edits to your photos. You can correct the brightness, contrast and color in a photo. You can straighten a tilted photo and remove scratches, blemishes or red eyes. You can also add effects and text to a photo.

One of *Picasa's* best features is its photo sharing capability. You can use the program to create a web album and publish your photos online. You can also turn your photos into collages and slideshows to view at home. You can print photos using *Picasa* to upload your photos directly to one of the popular online photo printers such as Snapfish, Shutterfly, Walmart and Walgreens.

This book will help you learn the basic operations of the *Picasa* program. You can download sample photos and start practicing right away with the various editing tools and learn more about how photos are organized in *Picasa*. Afterwards you can apply this knowledge to manage and edit your own photos. In *Chapter 7 Working on Your Own Photos* you can read more about this subject.

I wish you lots of fun with this book!

Yvette Huijsman
Studio Visual Steps

PS We welcome your comments and suggestions.
Our email address is: info@visualsteps.com

Visual Steps Newsletter

All Visual Steps books follow the same methodology: clear and concise step-by-step instructions with screenshots to demonstrate each task.
A complete list of all our books can be found on our website **www.visualsteps.com**
You can also sign up to receive our **free Visual Steps Newsletter**.
In this Newsletter you will receive periodic information by email regarding:
- the latest titles and previously released books;
- special offers, supplemental chapters, tips and free informative booklets.
Also, our Newsletter subscribers may download any of the documents listed on the web page **www.visualsteps.com/info_downloads**

When you subscribe to our Newsletter you can be assured that we will never use your email address for any purpose other than sending you the information as previously described. We will not share this address with any third-party. Each Newsletter also contains a one-click link to unsubscribe.

Introduction to Visual Steps™

The Visual Steps handbooks and manuals are the best instructional materials available for learning how to work with computers, mobile devices and software applications. Nowhere else will you find better support to help you get started with a *Windows* computer, *Mac*, iPad or other tablet, iPhone, the Internet or various software applications.

Properties of the Visual Steps books:
- **Comprehensible contents**
  Addresses the needs of the beginner or intermediate user for a manual written in simple, straight-forward English.
- **Clear structure**
  Precise, easy to follow instructions. The material is broken down into small enough segments to allow for easy absorption.
- **Screenshots of every step**
  Quickly compare what you see on your screen with the screenshots in the book. Pointers and tips guide you when new windows or alert boxes are opened so you always know what to do next.
- **Get started right away**
  All you have to do is turn on your computer or laptop and have your book at hand. Perform each operation as indicated on your own device.
- **Layout**
  The text is printed in a large size font and is clearly legible.

In short, I believe these manuals will be excellent guides for you.

Dr. H. van der Meij
Faculty of Applied Education, Department of Instructional Technology, University of Twente, the Netherlands

What You Will Need

To be able to work through this book, you will need a number of things:

  The main requirement for being able to work with this book is to have the *Picasa* program installed on your computer. In *Chapter 1 Setting up Picasa* you can read how to do this.

 Also, your computer needs to be using the *Windows* operating system. The screenshots in this book have been made on a *Windows 8.1* computer. But the book can also be used by people who own a *Windows 7* or *Windows Vista* computer.

You will need an active Internet connection in order to download the *Picasa* program and the practice files, among other things,

Furthermore, you will need to have:

 A printer to print photos at home. If you do not own a printer you can skip the print exercises.

 A digital photo camera, a portable device with a built-in camera or a scanner for transferring photos to your computer. In this book you will learn how to use the program by using a number of sample photos. In *Chapter 7 Working on Your Own Photos* you will learn how to transfer your own photos to the computer.

Your Basic Knowledge

This book has been written for computer users who have basic computer skills. If you do not have these skills, you can use one of our beginner's books on using *Windows*.

Windows 8 for SENIORS – ISBN 978 90 5905 118 8
www.visualsteps.com/windows8

Windows 7 for SENIORS – ISBN 978 90 5905 126 3
www.visualsteps.com/windows7

Windows Vista for SENIORS – ISBN 978 90 5905 274 1
www.visualsteps.com/vista

How to Use This Book

This book has been written using the Visual Steps™ method. The method is simple: just place the book next to your computer or laptop and perform each task step by step, directly on your own device. With the clear instructions and the multitude of screenshots, you will always know exactly what to do. This is the quickest way to become familiar with *Picasa*.

In this Visual Steps™ book, you will see various icons. This is what they mean:

Techniques
These icons indicate an action to be carried out:

  The mouse icon means you need to do something with the mouse.

  The keyboard icon means you should type something on your keyboard.

☞ The hand icon means you should do something else, for example, turn on the computer or carry out a task previously learned.

In some areas of this book additional icons indicate warnings or helpful hints. These will help you avoid mistakes and alert you when you need to make a decision about something.

Help
These icons indicate that extra help is available:

➥ The arrow icon warns you about something.

✖ The bandage icon will help you if something has gone wrong.

👣1 Have you forgotten how to do something? The number next to the footsteps tells you where to look it up at the end of the book in the appendix *How Do I Do That Again?*

The following icons indicate general information or tips. This information is displayed in separate boxes.

Extra information
Information boxes are denoted by these icons:

  The book icon gives you extra background information that you can read at your convenience. This extra information is not necessary for working through the book.

  The light bulb icon indicates an extra tip for using a program or service.

Website

On the website accompanying this book you can find the sample photos that are used in the book: **www.visualsteps.com/picasaseniors**
Be sure to check this website from time to time, to see if we have added any additional information or errata for this book.

Test Your Knowledge

After you have worked through a book, you can test your knowledge online, on the **www.ccforseniors.com** website. By answering a number of multiple choice questions you will be able to test your knowledge of *Picasa*. If you pass the test, you can also receive a free *Computer Certificate* by email.
Participating in the test is **free of charge**. The computer certificate website is a free service from Visual Steps.

For Teachers

This book is designed as a self-study guide. It is also well suited for use in a group or a classroom setting. For this purpose, we offer a free teacher's manual containing information about how to prepare for the course (including didactic teaching methods) and testing materials. You can download the teacher's manual (PDF file) from the website which accompanies this book: **www.visualsteps.com/picasaseniors**

The Screenshots

The screenshots used in this book indicate which button, folder, file or hyperlink you need to click on your computer screen. In the instruction text (in **bold** letters) you will see a small image of the item you need to click. The black line will point you to the right place on your screen.
The small screenshots that are printed in this book are not meant to be completely legible all the time. This is not necessary, as you will see these images on your own computer screen in real size and fully legible.

Here you see an example of an instruction text and a screenshot. The black line indicates where to find this item on your own computer screen:

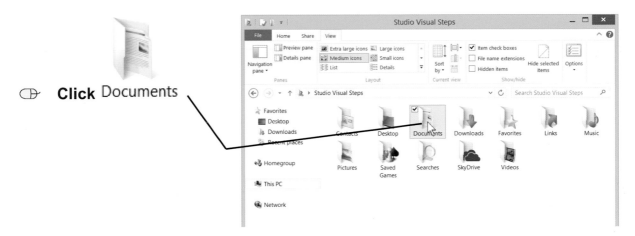

Sometimes the screenshot shows only a portion of a window. Here is an example:

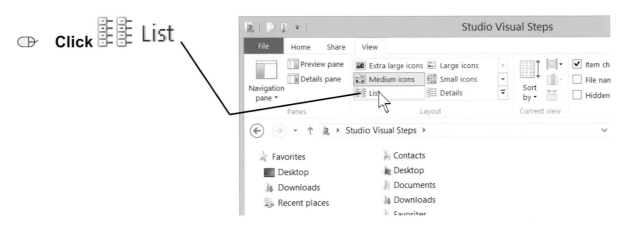

It really will **not be necessary** for you to read all the information in the screenshots in this book. Always use the screenshots in combination with the image you see on your own computer screen.

1. Setting up Picasa

Picasa, the photo editing program owned by *Google* since 2004, has become very popular. Not only is it available as a free download, it is loaded with many options and is simple to use. It also lends a feeling of extra security, knowing that no matter how many edits you make in *Picasa*, your original photos will always be preserved.

In this book you will learn how to use the various tools available in *Picasa* for editing photos. First, we start by showing you step by step how to download and install *Picasa*. There are also practice files available for this book. You can download both the *Picasa* program and the practice files from the Internet. If you use the practice files you will be certain that the images on your screen match the screenshots in this book. After you have learned how to use the program with the practice files you can start working on your own photos. In *Chapter 7 Working on Your Own Photos* you can read more about this.

Picasa uses its own system for ordering photos. You will see how this works by looking at the *Library*. When you open *Picasa* for the first time, your photos will automatically be included in this *Library*. In this chapter you will learn how to arrange your photos in folders, in *File Explorer* as well as in the *Picasa* albums. You will also learn how to navigate through the *Library*, how to view photos, and zoom in and out.

In this chapter you will learn how to:

- download and install *Picasa*;
- download the practice files with sample photos;
- open *Picasa* and select which folders *Picasa* should scan;
- use the *Library* and learn more about the layout of this window;
- organize photos in folders and in *File Explorer*;
- create, fill, and delete an album in *Picasa*;
- view photos and add captions to them;
- zoom in and zoom out;
- use the Photo Tray and Facial Recognition.

➥ Please note:

Picasa is updated on a regular basis. It is always possible that a particular option becomes available in another place, or a button changes its appearance. However, most of the main functions will remain the same. If your screen looks very different from the images in this book, be sure to visit **www.visualsteps.com/picasaseniors** This web page will give you information about any recent changes made to *Picasa*.

1.1 Downloading and Installing Picasa

If you want to install *Picasa* you need to download the program from the Internet first:

☞ **Open *Internet Explorer*** ¹

➥ **Please note:**
If you are using a *Windows 8.1* computer you need to open *Internet Explorer* from your desktop whenever you work with this book. Do not open with the tile shown in the *Apps* screen (Modern UI or Metro version of *Internet Explorer*).

☞ **Go to picasa.google.com** ₰²

Note that you do not need to type 'www' at the beginning of the web address.

You will see a brief explanation regarding *Picasa*:

↪ **Click**

Download Picasa

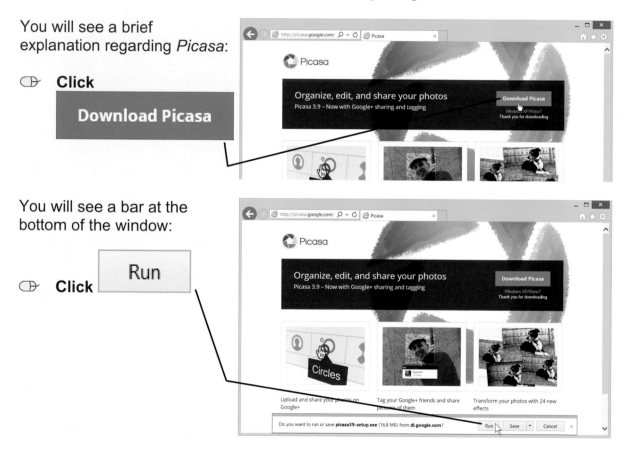

You will see a bar at the bottom of the window:

↪ **Click** | Run |

Your computer screen will turn dark and you will need to give permission to continue:

☞ **Give permission to continue** ₰³

A window will now be displayed where you need to agree to the terms and conditions:

At the bottom of the window:

☞ **Click**

I Agree

> agreement between you and Google. "Google" means Google Inc., whose principal place of business is at 1600 Amphitheatre Parkway, Mountain View, CA 94043, United
>
> If you accept the terms of the agreement, click I Agree to continue. You must accept the agreement to install Picasa 3.
>
> Nullsoft Install System v2.42.4-Unicode
>
> | Printable Version... | | I Agree | Cancel |

☞ **Click**

Install

> **Destination Folder**
>
> | C:\Program Files (x86)\Google\Picasa3 | Browse... |
>
> Space required: 66.5MB
> Space available: 873.2GB
>
> Nullsoft Install System v2.42.4-Unicode
>
> | < Back | Install | Cancel |

Just leave the checkmark ✔ by
Create Shortcut on Desk

☞ **Uncheck** ✔ **all the other options**

☞ **Click**

Finish

> **Picasa 3 Setup** — ☐ ✕
>
> **Completing the Picasa 3 Setup**
>
> Picasa 3 has been installed on your computer.
>
> Click Finish to close Setup.
>
> ☑ Create Shortcut on Desktop
>
> ☐ Add Shortcut to Quick Launch
>
> ☐ Set Google as my default search engine in Internet Explorer
>
> ☐ Send anonymous usage stats to Google
>
> Learn more about our privacy policy...
>
> ☐ Run Picasa 3
>
> | < Back | Finish | Cancel |

Now *Picasa* has been installed on your computer:

☞ **Close** *Internet Explorer* ⁴

You will see the *Picasa* icon on your desktop:

1.2 Downloading Sample Photos

In order to follow the exercises in this book you will need to use a number of sample photos. Here is how you download these photos:

☞ **Open *Internet Explorer* ᵍ1**

☞ **Open the web page www.visualsteps.com/picasaseniors ᵍ2**

🖱 **Click**
Practice files

🖱 **Click**
[Practice-Files.zip]

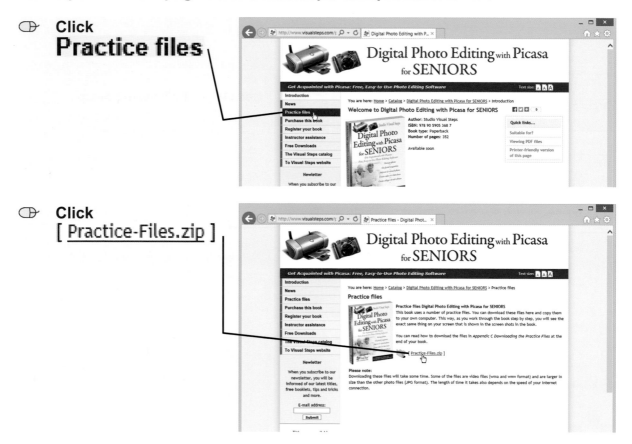

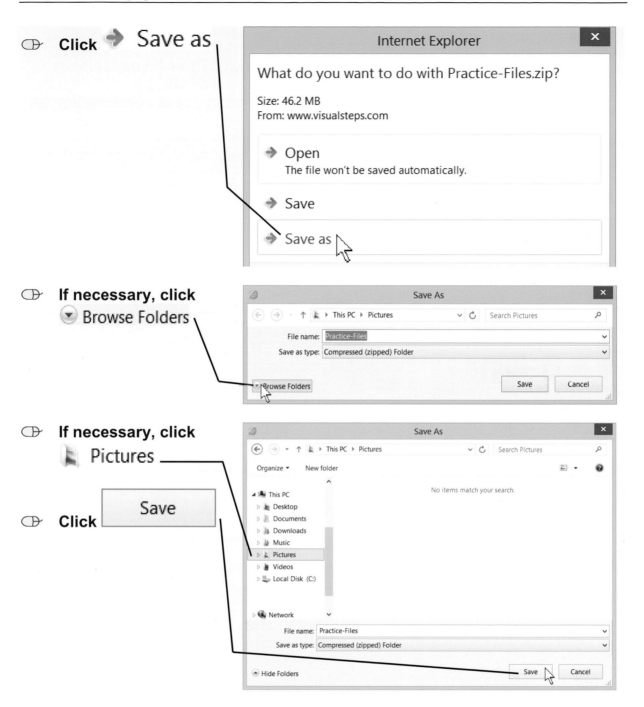

☞ **Click** ➡ Save as

☞ **If necessary, click** ▾ Browse Folders

☞ **If necessary, click** 🖼 Pictures

☞ **Click** Save

Once the entire file has been downloaded you will see *The download has completed* message:

⊙   **Click**   Open folder

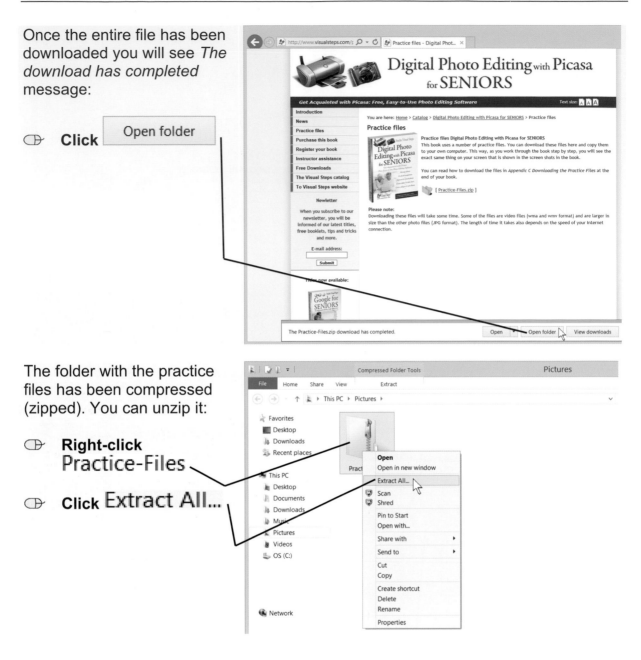

The folder with the practice files has been compressed (zipped). You can unzip it:

⊙   **Right-click** Practice-Files

⊙   **Click** Extract All...

☞ **Click**

The files will be unzipped.

Once the files have been
unzipped you will see a
number of photos as well as a
folder named 'Video':

You can move the folder with the practice video to the folder called (*My*) *Videos* on
your computer:

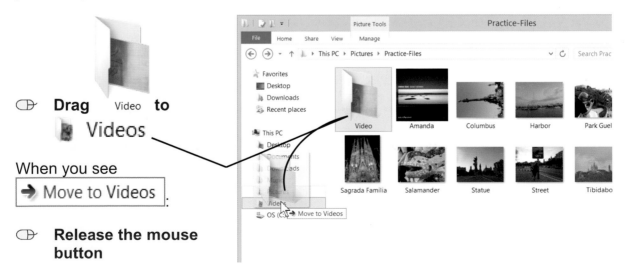

☞ **Drag** Video **to**

     Videos

When you see
→ Move to Videos :

☞ **Release the mouse
button**

You can move the sound file as well:

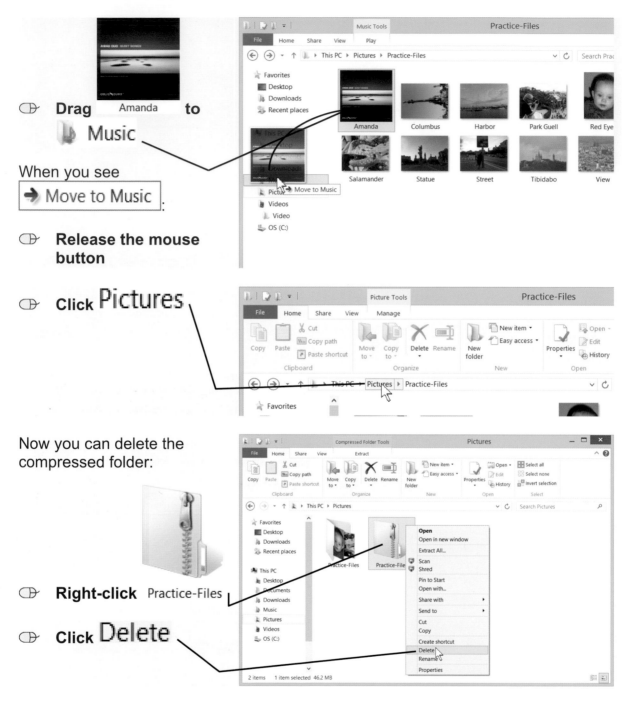

⊕ **Drag** Amanda **to** 🎵 Music

When you see ➡ Move to Music :

⊕ **Release the mouse button**

⊕ **Click** Pictures

Now you can delete the compressed folder:

⊕ **Right-click** Practice-Files

⊕ **Click** Delete

You may need to confirm that you want to delete the folder:

⊕ **Click** [Yes]

The compressed folder has been deleted.

☞ **Close the open windows** ᵍᵍ4

The exercises in this book are all based on these practice files. If you use these files as you work through this book, the images on your screen should match the screenshots in the book.

1.3 Opening Picasa

You can open *Picasa* in several ways. The easiest way is by using the icon on your desktop. On the desktop:

☞ **Double-click** Picasa 3

When you open *Picasa* for the first time, the program will want to search your computer for photos. The photos that have been found will not be moved or copied; they will only be displayed in the *Picasa Library*. You can choose whether you want to search the whole computer or just your own folders:

☞ **Click the radio button**

    ◉ **by**

Only search My D

☞ **Click**

    Continue

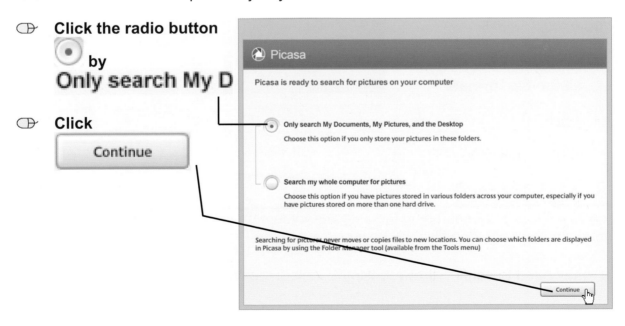

💡 Tip

Which folders do you search?

You have stored the sample photos in the *(My) Pictures* folder. This folder will be found if you have carried out the actions as described above. When you start working through *section 1.5 Photos and Folders in File Explorer*, the images on your screen should match the screenshots in this book.

The `Search my whole computer for pictures` option is not recommended. This option will also display photos belonging to other users of your computer, and other types of images as well. For example, icons, symbols, and images from web pages saved on your computer by *Internet Explorer* (or other browser application). There may be thousands of images to collect if you choose this option and it will take a long time to do it.

The *Picasa* program includes a photo viewer. This is a program with which you can open and view photos on your computer. When you open *Picasa* for the first time, you can set this viewer as the default photo viewer for all your photos:

The default viewer option is enabled:

All file formats have been selected:

If your own computer displays different settings:

☞ **Check the box ☑ by all the file formats**

☞ **Click**

Finish

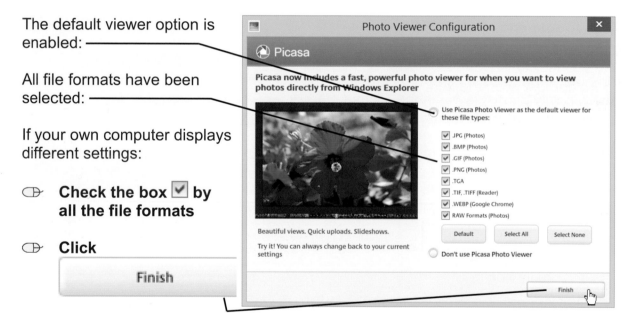

Picasa will now start searching the selected folders on your computer. Folders that contain images or video files will be displayed in the *Picasa Library*.

You may see this window:

☞ **If necessary, click**

Not now

🐦 **Please note:**

If you have saved any of your own photos in the *(My) Pictures* or *(My) Documents* folders, or on your desktop, these will also be displayed in *Picasa*. In the next section you will be selecting the folders that will be displayed in *Picasa*, in order to match the images on your screen to the images in this book.

The photos found by *Picasa* will be displayed in the start screen. This is called the *Library*.

The *Folder List* is on the left-hand side: ─────

The *Lightbox* is on the right-hand side of the screen:

The *Photo Tray* is on the bottom:

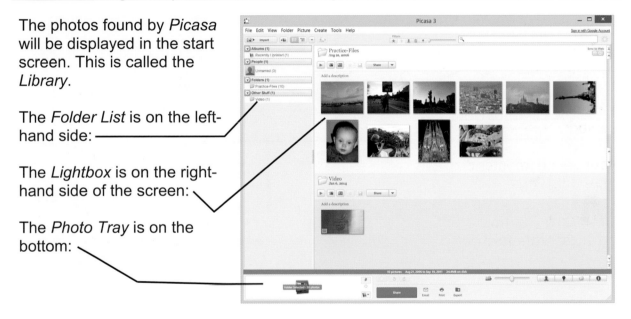

- In this example, the *Folder List* on the left-hand side of the *Library* contains just one folder. A folder is a storage location on your computer. The photos in the folders are ordered by the date the photos were made.
- The *Lightbox* on the right-hand side of the *Library* displays a thumbnail overview. Thumbnails are miniature pictures of the photos found by *Picasa*, per folder. You will see the name of the folder and the date of the first photo.
- The *Photo Tray* lets you collect photos from one or more folders or albums so that you can work with them as a group.

➥ **Please note:**

In the Folder List you will only see the name of the folder that actually contains the photo. If a photo has been saved in a subfolder, the only name that is displayed is the name of the last (sub)folder; you will not see the name of the folder to which this subfolder belongs.

1.4 Folder Manager

The program will continuously search for images in the (*My*) *Pictures* and (*My*) *Documents* folders, and on the desktop. This process is called *scanning*. Any changes made to a folder stored on your computer will affect the folders shown in *Picasa* as well. With the *Folder Manager* you can select the folders that will be scanned and thereby determine which folders can be displayed in *Picasa*.

If you want to delete a folder from *Picasa* but not from your computer, you will need to do this:

☞ **Click** Tools

☞ **Click**
Folder Manager...

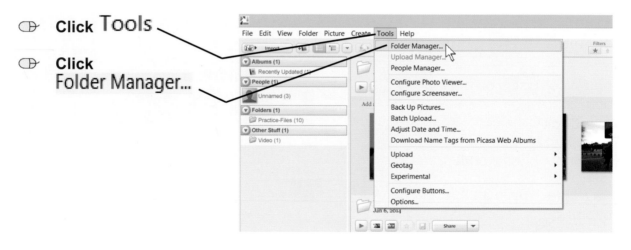

The C icon appears next to the folders you have allowed to be scanned:

The folders that are not scanned are indicated by an **✗** :

> **Folder Manager**
>
> **Folder List**
> - C ▦ Desktop
> - ▷ C 🖼 My Pictures
> - ▷ C 🚪 My Documents
> - ▷ ✗ 💾 C:\
> - ▷ ✗ 💾 P:\
> - ▷ ✗ 💾 R:\
> - ▷ ✗ 💾 T:\
>
> For each folder, you can choose whether or not to have Picasa find pictures inside it. You can also pick folders to watch for new pictures.
>
> **For the current folder:**
> - ✓ Scan Once
> - ✗ Remove from Picasa
> - C Scan Always
> - 👤 Face Detection On
>
> **Watched Folders**
> My Pictures
> My Documents
> Desktop
> My Videos
>
> [OK] [Cancel] [Help]

Now you are going to change the settings. This is because you want the folder with the practice files to be the only folder that is scanned:

☞ **Click** ▦ Desktop

☞ **Click** ✗ Remove from Picasa

☞ **Click** 🖼 My Pictures

☞ **Click** ✗ Remove from Picasa

☞ **Click** 🚪 My Documents

☞ **Click** ✗ Remove from Picasa

> **Folder Manager**
>
> **Folder List**
> - ✗ ▦ Desktop
> - ▷ ✗ 🖼 My Pictures
> - ▶ C 🚪 My Documents
> - ▷ ✗ 💾 C:\
> - ▷ ✗ 💾 P:\
> - ▷ ✗ 💾 R:\
> - ▷ ✗ 💾 T:\
>
> For each folder, you can choose whether or not to have Picasa find pictures inside it. You can also pick folders to watch for new pictures.
>
> **For the current folder:**
> - ✓ Scan Once
> - ✗ Remove from Picasa
> - ● C Scan Always
> - 👤 Face Detection On
>
> **Watched Folders**
> My Documents
> My Videos
>
> [OK] [Cancel] [Help]

Now all folders show an **✗** beside the folder name. You may notice one folder remaining on the scan list, namely the (*My*) *Videos* folder.

If this is the case, you can delete this folder like this:

☞ **By Watched Folders,** click **My Videos**

☞ **Click ✖ Remove from Picasa**

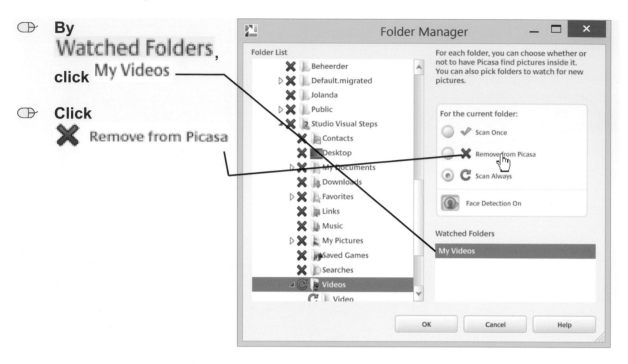

Now all folders show an ✖ next to the folder name. The folder containing the practice files is a subfolder of the *(My) Pictures* folder. Here is how to display this subfolder:

☞ **Drag the scroll bar upwards**

☞ **If necessary, click ▷ by My Pictures**

☞ **Click Practice-Files**

☞ **Click ↻ Scan Always**

By **Practice-Files** you will see that the ✖ icon turns into a ↻.

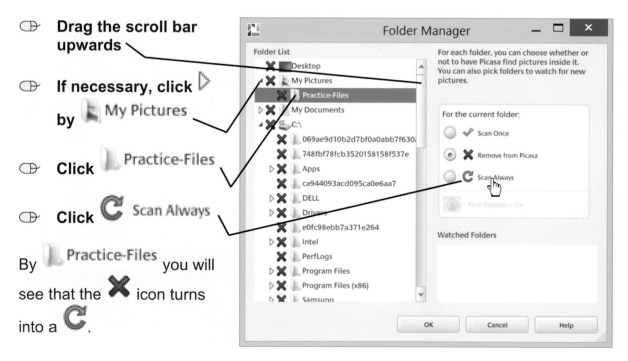

If **Watched Folders** contains other folders than the
My Pictures\Practice-Files :

⊕ **Click the folder**

⊕ **Click** ✖ Remove from Picasa

If you see just **My Pictures\Practice-Files** by **Watched Folders** :

At the bottom of the window:

⊕ **Click** [OK]

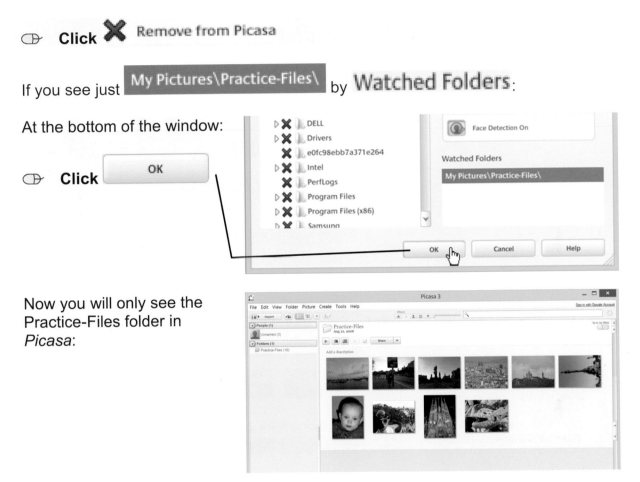

Now you will only see the
Practice-Files folder in
Picasa:

💡 **Tip**

Your own photos
As you work through this book you will be using the sample photos from the
Practice-Files folder that you downloaded earlier. Once you have worked through all
the chapters and want to get started with your own photos, you can use the *Folder
Manager* to add the folders that contain your own photos, and hide the folder
containing the practice files.

In *Chapter 7 Working with Your Own Photos* you can read how to use *Picasa* to
transfer photos from your camera to your computer.

1.5 Photos and Folders in File Explorer

You can take a look at the folder that will be displayed in *Picasa* using *File Explorer*. You can switch to *File Explorer* while you are in *Picasa*:

☞ **Click**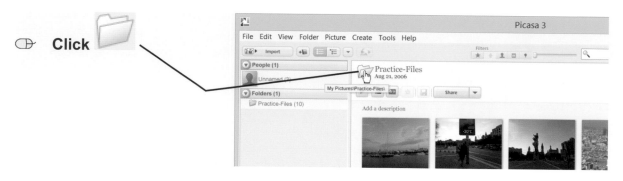

You will see the familiar *File Explorer* window containing the sample photos. You can use *File Explorer* to create a new folder like this:

In *Windows 8.1*:

☞ **If necessary, click** ⌄

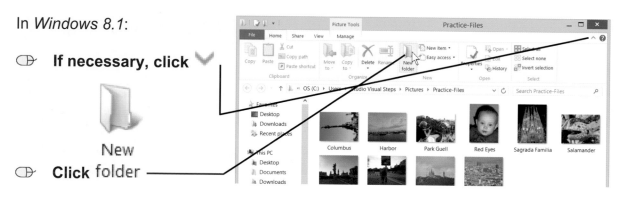

☞ **Click folder**

In *Windows 7* and *Vista* you need to right-click an empty section of the window and then in the small context menu that appears, click **New**, ⏶ **Folder** .

Enter a name for the new folder:

⌨ **Type:** Gaudi

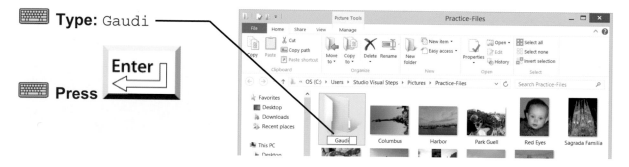

⌨ **Press** **Enter**

Now you can practice moving a few photos to this new folder. First, you need to select the photos that are to be moved:

Press Ctrl **and hold it down**

Click the photos named Park Guell, Sagrada Familia and Salamander

Release Ctrl

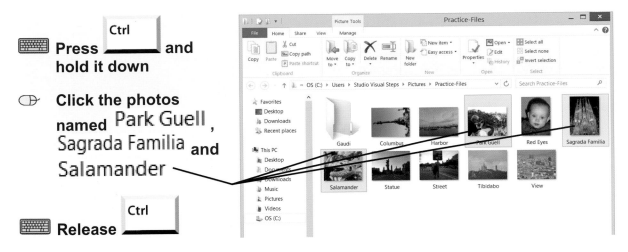

The three photos have been selected. Move the photos to the new folder:

Drag the photos to

Gaudi

When you see ➡ Move to Gaudi.

Release the mouse button

Now the photos have been placed in the *Gaudi* folder:

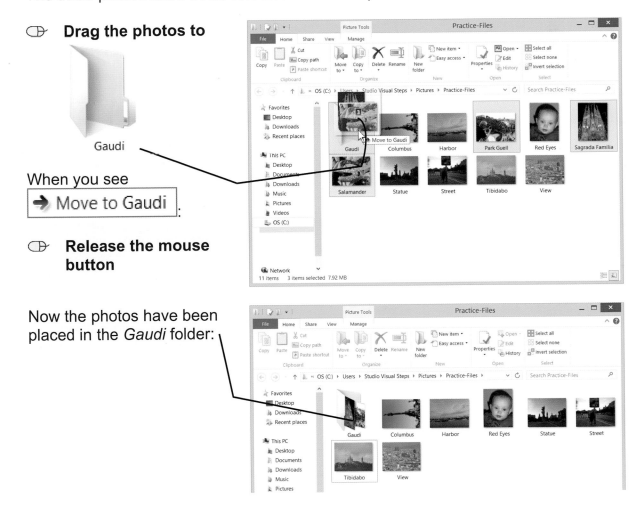

💡 Tip
Copying

If you keep holding the **Ctrl** key pressed down while dragging the photos, they will be copied instead of moved.

Now you can create another folder:

☞ **Create a new folder and call it** Red Eyes 🐾5

☞ **Move the photo called *Red Eyes* to the new folder** 🐾6

Now the *Practice-Files* folder contains two subfolders:

Close *File Explorer*:

👆 **Click** ❌

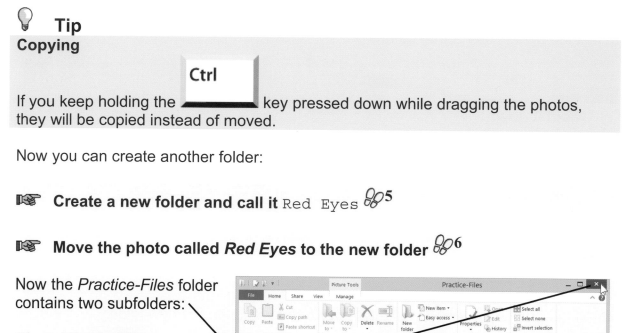

When you change anything in *File Explorer*, the change will be reflected in *Picasa*:

Now the Folder List contains three folders:

The *Practice-Files folder* and the two subfolders called *Gaudi* and *Red Eyes*. *Picasa* will display these folders separately:

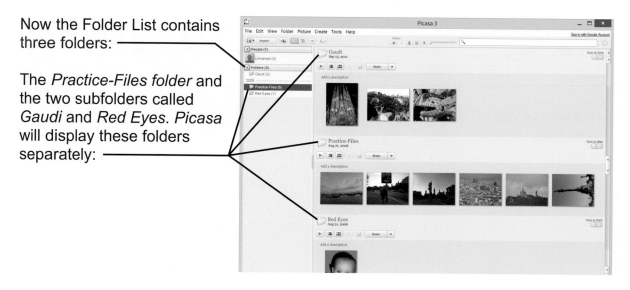

1.6 Albums in Picasa

You cannot create new folders in the *Picasa* program itself. This can only be done in *File Explorer*. But you can collect photos from one or more folders and save them in an *album*. An album is a *virtual* group of photos that only exists within the *Picasa* software. An album contains the links to the locations of the photos on your computer. The physical photos are not actually moved to an album; they are simply *displayed* in the album. This is how you create an album:

☞ **Click** File

☞ **Click** New Album...

Enter an identifiable name for the album:

⌨ **Type:** Practice Album

You do not need to fill in the other data.

☞ **Click** OK

The album called *Practice Album* is created:

In the Folder List you will see the new 🗔 Practice Album (0) album, by 🔽 **Albums (1)**.

The album does not yet contain any photos. This is how you add a photo to an album:

☞ **Right-click the cathedral photo**

☞ **Click**
Add to Album

☞ **Click**
Practice Album

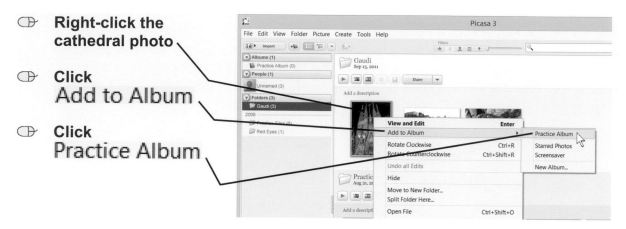

Now try adding a photo from a different folder:

☞ **Right-click the harbor photo**

☞ **Click**
Add to Album

☞ **Click**
Practice Album

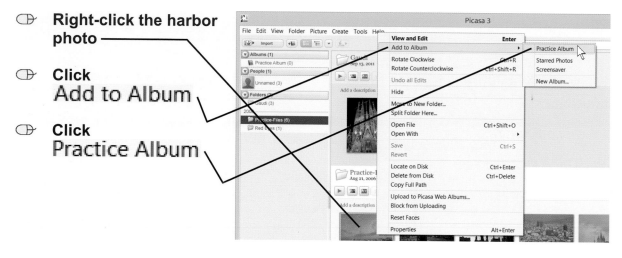

Open the album named *Practice Album*:

☞ **Click**
Practice Album (2)

You will see both photos in the album:

Note that an album is

indicated by the ▮ icon,

and a folder by ▭ :

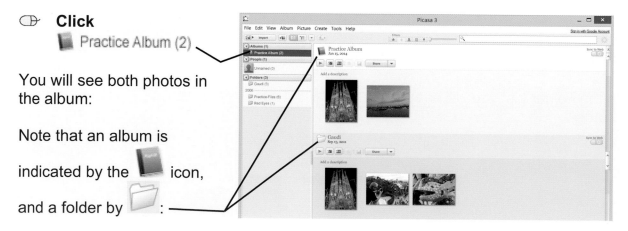

The album only contains the links to the photos that are stored in several folders. You will not be able to see the *Picasa* albums in *File Explorer*. Test this for yourself:

☞ **By** Gaudi **, click** 📁

The content of the *Gaudi* folder has not changed:

☞ **Click** Practice-Files

In the *Practice-Files folder* you will just see the photos and subfolders you previously created:

The album called *Practice Album* is not visible here.

Close *File Explorer*:

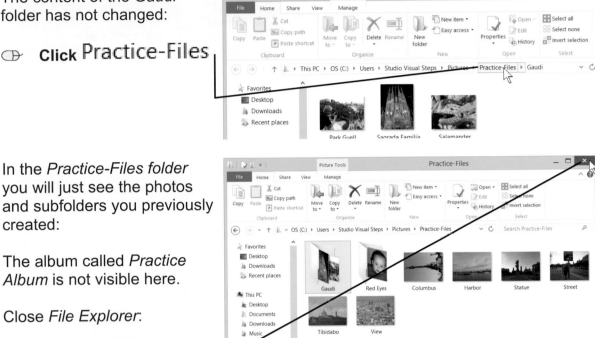

☞ **Click** ❌

If you delete photos in an album, or delete an entire album, the original photo files will still remain in their original folders. This is how you remove the cathedral photo from the *Practice Album*:

☞ **Click the photo**

⌨ **Press** Delete

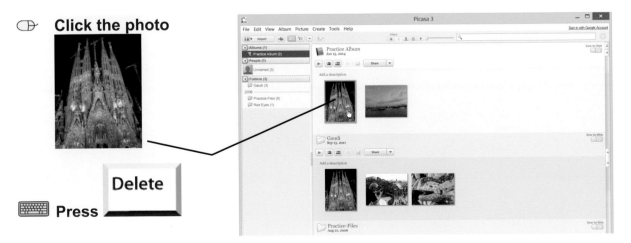

You will need to confirm this action:

☞ **Click**

   Remove Image

💡 Tip

Delete a photo from a folder

Photos that are deleted in this way will also be deleted from the albums where you have placed them. You will see a similar window:

The difference is that a photo that is deleted from a folder is also deleted from your computer. The photo will be moved to the *Recycle Bin*. You can still retrieve a photo from the *Recycle Bin*, if you wish.

Delete the *Practice Album*:

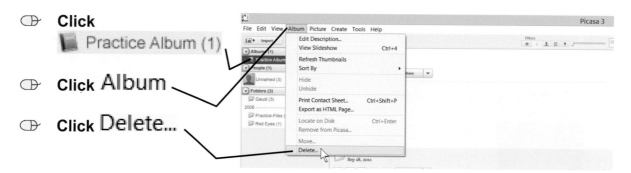

☞ **Click**
   Practice Album (1)

☞ **Click** Album

☞ **Click** Delete...

You will need to confirm this action:

Click   **Delete Album**

The album has been deleted. Now you will only see folders in *Picasa*.

➤ **Please note:**

It is best not to delete folders in the *Picasa* program. If you delete a folder in *Picasa*, for example, by clicking **Folder, Delete...**, this folder will also be deleted from the computer.
If this happens by accident, you can check if the folder is still present in the *Recycle*

Restore the

Bin. If this is the case, you can select the folder and click selected items. The folder will then be restored to its previous place in *File Explorer*. You can restore individual photos in the same way.

1.7 Viewing Photos

In the Lightbox you can search for your photos and view them. To take a look at a photo:

➤ **Double-click the photo**

You will see the photo in the viewing pane:

Below the photo you will see more information about it:

Gaudi > Park Guell.JPG   9/18/2011 1:32:26
2560x1920 pixels   2.8MB   (2 of 3)

💡 **Tip**

Resolution

The *resolution* of the photo is indicated by 2560x1920 pixels . The resolution is defined by the number of *pixels* (image dots) that make up the photo. The quality of the photo depends on the number of dots used. If a large number of dots are used to build up a photo, the photo will be very detailed (sharp). If there are fewer dots in the picture, the photo will be grainy and not so well-defined.

The higher the resolution, the larger you can print this photo without making it unclear. A photo with a low resolution will quickly become grainy and unclear when you enlarge it. You will often see the individual pixels, which makes it blurry.

Please note: once a picture has been taken, the resolution of the photo can no longer be altered. If you already know you want to enlarge or enhance and edit certain photos you need to make sure your camera has been set to take high-resolution photos. Read your camera manual or ask your retailer for more information about the settings on your camera.

A high-resolution photo will take up more memory space than a photo with a lower resolution. Fortunately, the capacity on the memory cards available these days has increased so much that you should easily have enough storage space to save lots of high-resolution photos.

1.8 Zooming In and Zooming Out

In *Picasa* you can zoom in to the photo's true size with a single command. This is the largest possible rendering of the photo where the photo quality will still be good. This is how you do it:

☞ **Click** [1:1]

Now the photo has been enlarged. You will only see a small part of the photo:

But the photo will still be sharp if you zoom in to this size.

You can zoom in even further:

⊕   **Drag the slider** by **all the way to the right**

In the selection frame you can see which part of the photo is displayed:

In the selection frame you can select the part of the photo you want to see:

⊕   **Click the man's face**

Now you will clearly see that the photo has become blurry and grainy due to the extreme enlargement:

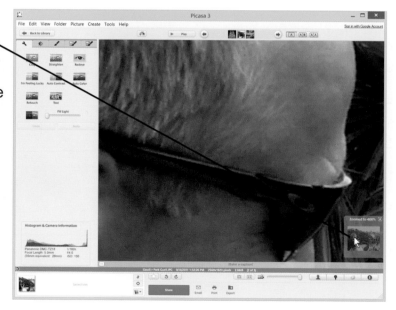

Zoom out again:

⊕ **Drag the slider 🖱 by 📷 to the left until this point**

You will see a larger part of the photo:

To see the full photo in the viewing area again:

⊕ **Click** 🔲

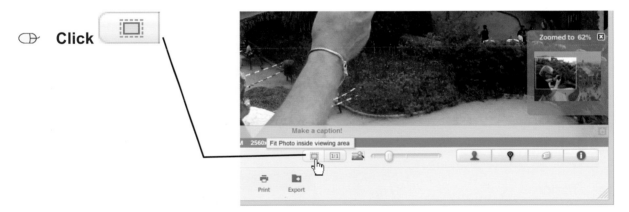

Now you see the entire picture. This is how to leaf back to the first photo in the folder:

⊕ **Click** ⬅

HELP! I do not see the 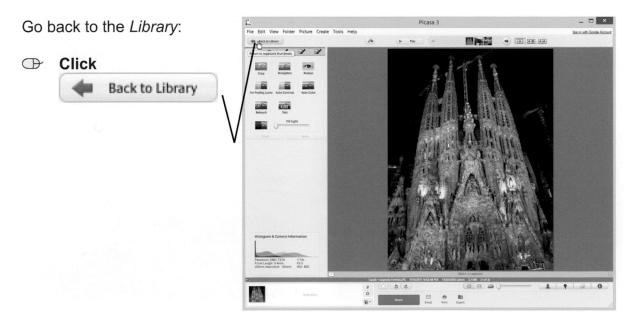 button.

If the button is not visible, you are probably already viewing the first photo in the folder. Go on to the next step.

You will see the photo of the Sagrada Familia:

In this example you cannot go back any further, because this is the first photo in the folder:

But you can go forward, with

the button:

HELP! I see a different picture.

If you do not see the photo of the Sagrada Familia, click or until you see the photo.

Go back to the *Library*:

◯ **Click**

Back to Library

You will see the photos in the *Gaudi* folder. In order to view a photo that is stored in another folder, you first need to click the folder in the Folder List:

☞ **Click the**
📁 Red Eyes (1)
folder

You will see the photo in this folder:

1.9 Adding a Caption

You can also add a caption (a title) to your photo. A photo caption is different from a file name. A caption is only visible in *Picasa*. A file name is the name of the photo file that is displayed in *File Explorer*. A caption provides extra information about the photo in *Picasa*. It is displayed below the thumbnail of the photo. Adding captions in *Picasa* also makes it easier to find a specific photo. Here is how you add a caption:

☞ **Open the salamander**
photo 🦶⁷

Below the photo:

☞ **Click**
Make a caption!

⌨ **Type:** Salamander by Gaudi

☞ **Click**
⬅ Back to Library
twice

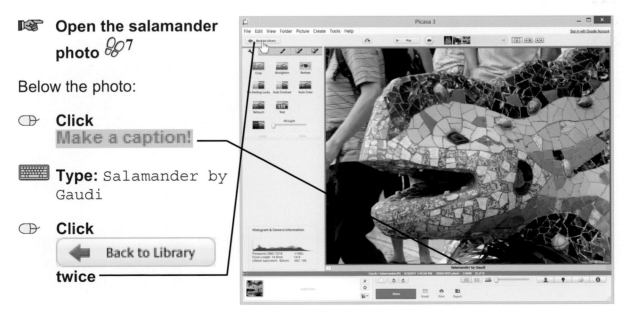

In the overview the photo
does not yet have a caption:

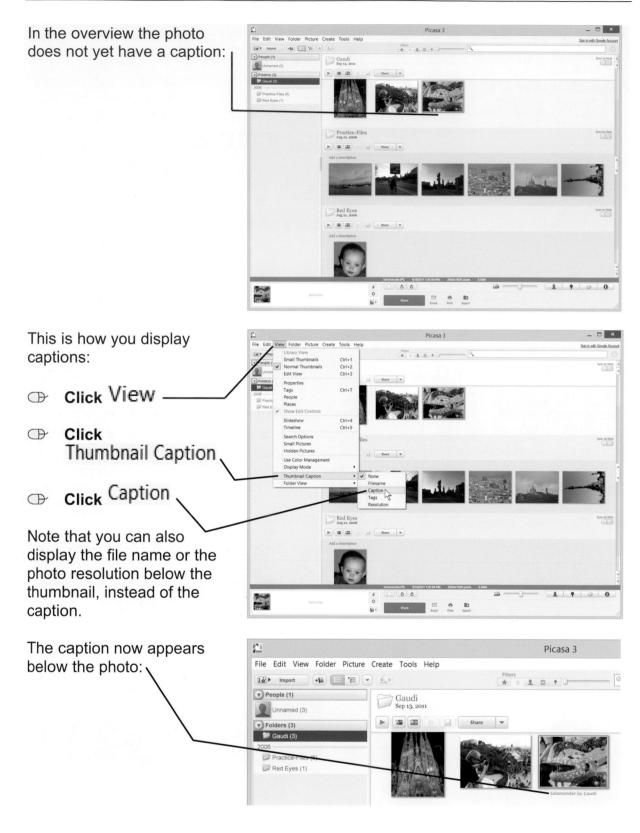

This is how you display
captions:

⊕ **Click** View

⊕ **Click**
   Thumbnail Caption

⊕ **Click** Caption

Note that you can also
display the file name or the
photo resolution below the
thumbnail, instead of the
caption.

The caption now appears
below the photo:

1.10 Using the Photo Tray

The Photo Tray is a kind of holding area. By collecting one or more photos there, you can perform various actions on the group of photos at once. These actions include printing, sending by email and moving. This is how you select two photos from the same folder:

Press Ctrl **and hold it down**

Click two photos in the *Practice-Files* folder

Release Ctrl

Now the photos have been placed in the Photo Tray:

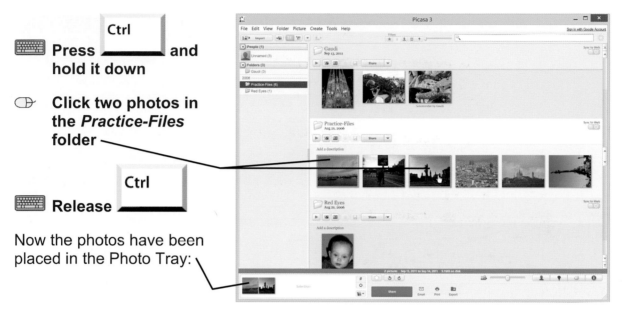

If you want to select some more photos from a different folder you will need to pin the first two photos to the tray first, otherwise they will disappear when you click another photo:

Click

Select one more photo:

☞ **If necessary, click**
  📁 Red Eyes (1)

☞ **Click the baby photo**

Now there are three photos in
the Photo Tray:

💡 Tip

Drag photos
If you drag the photos you want to select to the Photo Tray they will be pinned
automatically.

Now you can send these three photos by email, all at once, or you can print them or
share them online in a web album. In *Chapter 4 Fun and Useful Extras in Picasa*,
Chapter 5 Sharing Photos Online, and *Chapter 6 Printing Photos* you can learn how
to do this.

You can also edit the three photos you have selected:

☞ **Double-click the first
  photo**

The photo will be displayed in the viewing pane:

With the and buttons you can leaf through the three selected photos, in order to edit them separately:

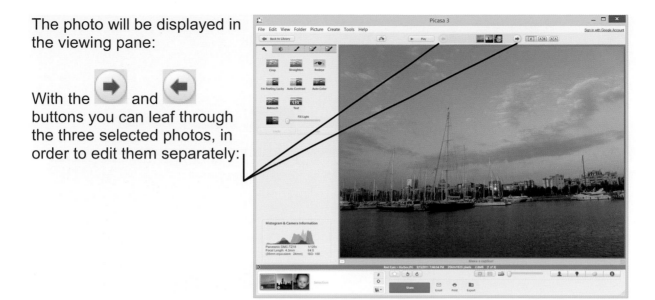

This is how you empty the Photo Tray:

☞ **Click a blank spot in the Photo Tray**

☞ **Click** ◯

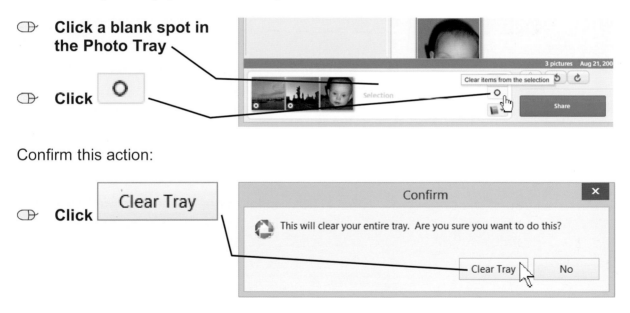

Confirm this action:

☞ **Click** Clear Tray

Now the Photo Tray is empty again.

1.11 Using Facial Recognition

Picasa will immediately scan the images for human faces. The faces that have been found will be placed in the **People (1)** folder. If you add a name to these faces it will be easier to find photos of the same person later on.

☞ **Click**

You might see the following screen:

☞ **Click** Close

Welcome to the Unnamed people album!

As Picasa scans your photos, the faces it finds are automatically grouped for easy naming.

Things to know:

To identify a person, click 'Add a name', then type in the person's name and press Enter. A new People album will be created each time you name someone for the first time.

(TIP: Sign in with your Google Account to gain access to all of your Google Account contacts while naming.)

To ignore a person, click the 'X' button on the face thumbnail.

Suggestions: After you name someone, Picasa may suggest more matching faces for that person. Click on a person's album to view and confirm (or reject) any suggestions.

You can upload name tags to Picasa Web Albums. Photos uploaded or 'Synced to Web' will carry the name tags you've provided.

Click 'Learn More' for information about this feature.

Learn more...   Close

You will see the faces that have been found:

🩹 HELP! I do not see as many faces.

If you see fewer faces than in this example, you need to click the *Expand Groups* button:

☞ **Click** | Expand groups |

You can add a *name tag* (keyword) to a photo:

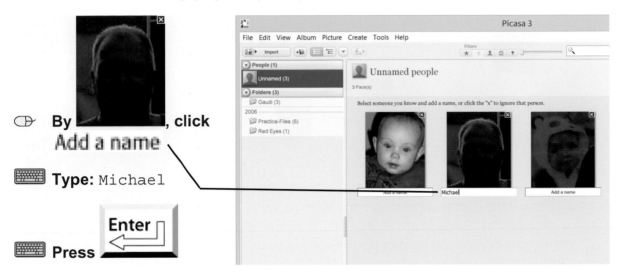

☞ **By** [image], **click** Add a name

⌨ **Type:** Michael

⌨ **Press** | Enter ⏎ |

You will see a new window with the name in it:

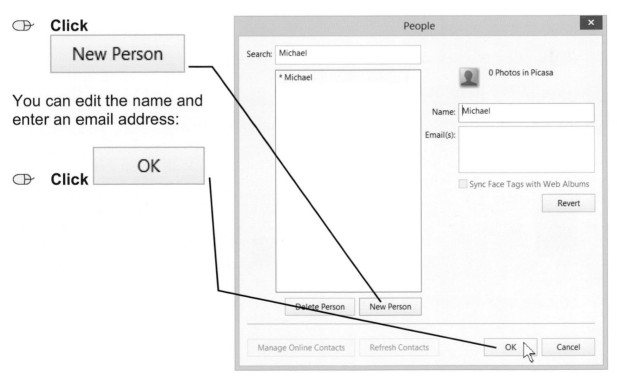

☞ **Click** | New Person |

You can edit the name and enter an email address:

☞ **Click** | OK |

Now the photo has disappeared from the album of unnamed people:

A *People* album has been created for Michael

Michael (1)

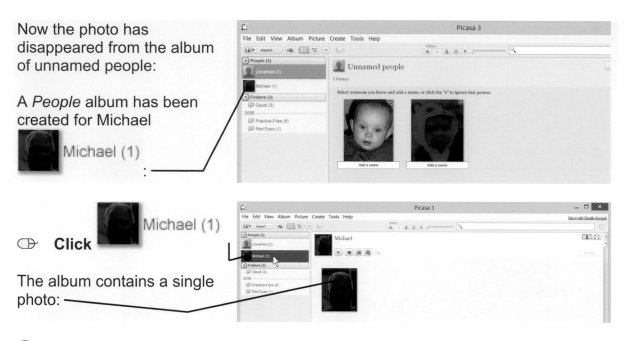

☞ **Click** Michael (1)

The album contains a single photo:

💡 Tip

More photos of the same person
In this example, the *People* album only contains one picture of Michael. If your own photo collection contains multiple photos of the same person, you can add these photos to his or her 'people album', like this:

☞ **If necessary, click** Unnamed

☞ **Right-click the desired photo**

☞ **Click** Move to People Album

☞ **Click the name you want to use, for example** Michael

If you want to delete the name tag for a specific photo, you do that like this:

☞ **Right-click** Michael (1)

☞ **Click** Edit People Album...

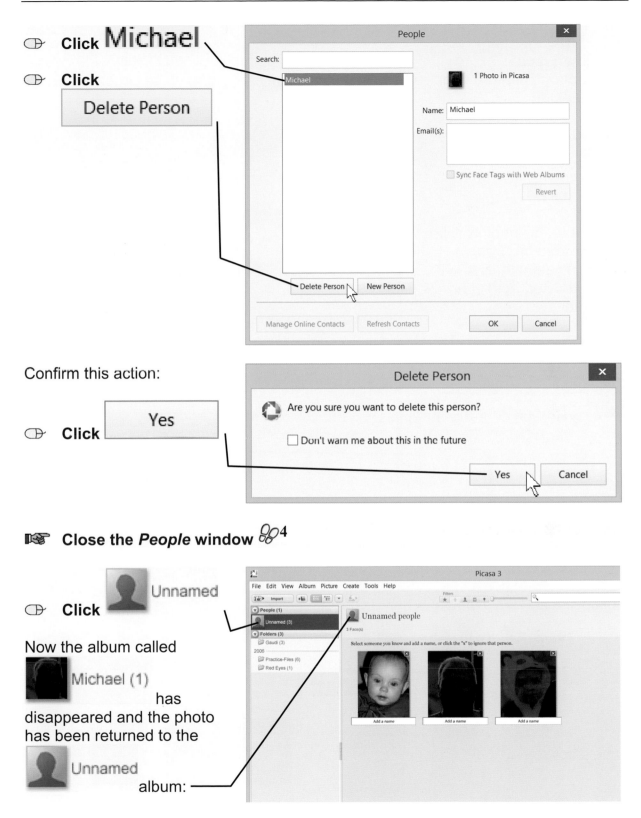

☞ **Click** Michael

☞ **Click** Delete Person

Confirm this action:

☞ **Click** Yes

☞ **Close the *People* window** 📖⁴

☞ **Click** Unnamed

Now the album called Michael (1) has disappeared and the photo has been returned to the Unnamed album:

💡 Tip

Unknown faces

If your photos feature people you do not know, you can ignore these people in the *People* album:

By the photo you want to ignore:

☞ **Click ⊠**

The link to this photo will be deleted from the *People* album. The photo itself will not be deleted from your computer.

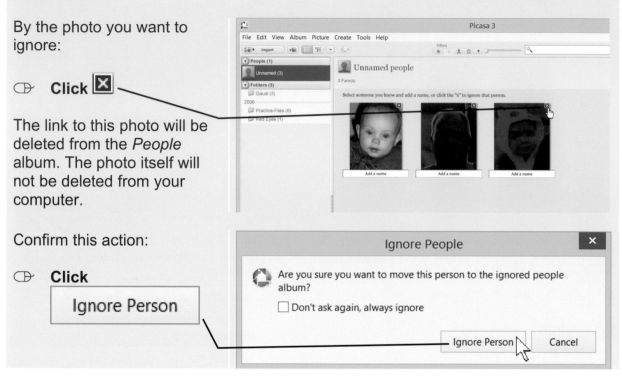

Confirm this action:

☞ **Click**

Ignore Person

💡 Tip

Disable Facial Recognition

If you do not want to use the *Facial Recognition* function at all, you can disable it. In the *Tips* at the end of this chapter you can read how to do that.

Collapse the *People* album:

☞ **By People (1), click**
▼

You will see the sample photos again:

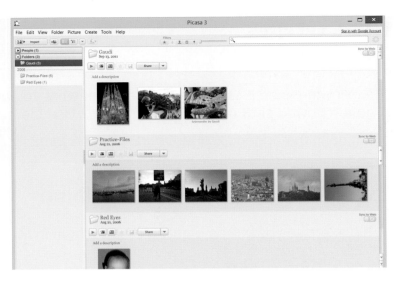

☞ **Close** *Picasa* 🐾⁴

By now you have learned the main methods for using the *Picasa Library*. In the next few exercises you can repeat these actions and practice some more. In the next chapter you will learn how to edit the photos.

1.12 Exercises

🐾

The following exercises will help you master what you have just learned. Have you forgotten how to perform a particular action? Use the number beside the footsteps to look it up in the appendix *How Do I Do That Again?* 🐾[1]

Exercise 1: Creating a New Album

In this exercise you will be creating a new album in *Picasa*.

☞ Open *Picasa*. 🐾[8]

☞ Create a new album and call it *Practice Album*. 🐾[11]

☞ Add the salamander photo to the album called *Practice Album*. 🐾[12]

☞ Add the baby photo to the album called *Practice Album*. 🐾[12]

☞ Open the album named *Practice Album*. 🐾[9]

☞ Delete the baby photo from the album. 🐾[13]

☞ Delete the album named *Practice Album*. 🐾[14]

☞ Close *Picasa*. 🐾[4]

Exercise 2: Zooming In and Out

In this exercise you will open a photo and practice zooming in and out.

☞ Open *Picasa*. 🐾[8]

☞ Open the photo of the harbor. 🐾[7]

☞ View the photo in its true size. 🐾[15]

☞ Display the bow of the big ship. 🐾[16]

☞ Zoom in on the photo as far as you can. 🦶**17**

☞ Zoom out a little bit. 🦶**18**

☞ Adjust the size of the photo so that it fits in the viewing pane. 🦶**19**

☞ Go back to the *Library* 🦶**20** and close *Picasa*. 🦶**4**

1.13 Background Information

Dictionary

Album	Albums are virtual groups of photos that only exist within the *Picasa* software. You can combine photos in one album, and you can use a single photo in multiple albums without taking up any extra disk space. If you delete photos in an album or delete the entire album, the original photo files will still be saved.
Facial Recognition	A function for which *Picasa* uses Facial Recognition techniques to scan people's faces, so you can add name tags to them.
Folder List	An overview of all the folders on your computer containing photos, and of all the albums you have created. The Folder List is displayed on the left-hand side of the *Library*.
Library	A window that presents an overview of all the photos, folders and albums in *Picasa*.
Lightbox	An overview of thumbnail pictures of your photos, shown on the right-hand side of the *Library* in the Lightbox.
(Name) tag	A keyword you can add to a photo.
People album	For each name tag you have added with the *Facial Recognition* function, an album will be created and named after the person in the photo. This album contains the photos you have identified as this person.
Photo Tray	The Photo Tray allows you to collect photos as a group so that you can perform certain actions on the group at once, such as printing, sending by email or moving.
Viewing pane	A window in which an opened photo is displayed. On the left-hand side of this window you will see an assortment of buttons and tabs that can be used to perform various photo editing options.

Source: Picasa Help

1.14 Tips

💡 Tip

Use the scroll bar

The scroll bar in the Lightbox works a bit differently from the usual *Windows* scroll bars.

To scroll through folders:

👉 **Click** ⏶ **or** ⏷

To scroll through photos:

👉 **Click** ⏶ **or** ⏷

To scroll manually:

👉 **Drag the scroll box downwards or upwards**

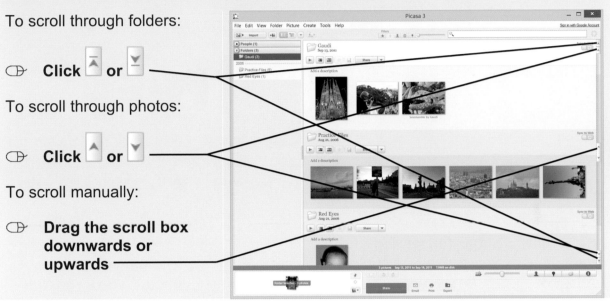

💡 Tip

Change the sorting order

By default, the folders are sorted by their date of creation. But you can choose a different sorting order:

In the top left-hand corner of the window:

👉 **Click** ⏷

👉 **Click the desired order**

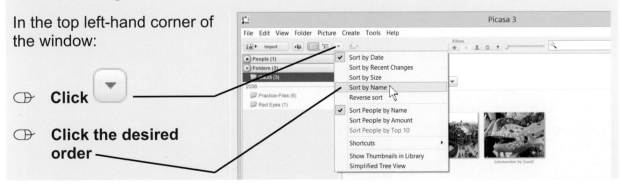

💡 Tip

Smaller thumbnails
If you have a lot of folders and photos you can set the thumbnails to be even smaller. This means you will see more photos on your screen.

☞ **Click View**

☞ **Click Small Thumbnails**

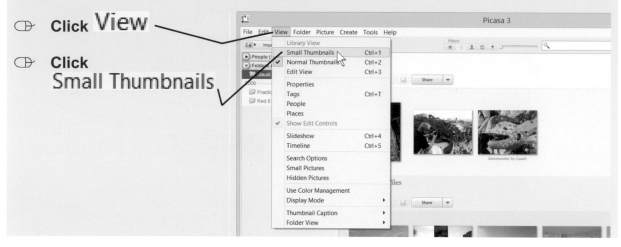

💡 Tip

Briefly view a photo full screen
In the Lightbox you can view a photo on a full screen for a brief moment:

☞ **Place the mouse pointer on a photo in the Lightbox**

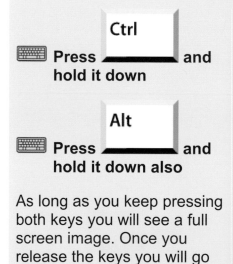

Press Ctrl and hold it down

Press Alt and hold it down also

As long as you keep pressing both keys you will see a full screen image. Once you release the keys you will go back to the Lightbox.

Tip

Disable Facial Recognition

Picasa will automatically look for faces in the photos that are displayed in the program. This process may take quite a bit of time if your computer contains many photos. This is how you disable the *Facial Recognition* function:

☞ **Click** Tools

☞ **Click** Options...

☞ **Click the** Name Tags **tab**

☞ **Uncheck the box** ☑ **by** Enable face detection

☞ **Click** OK

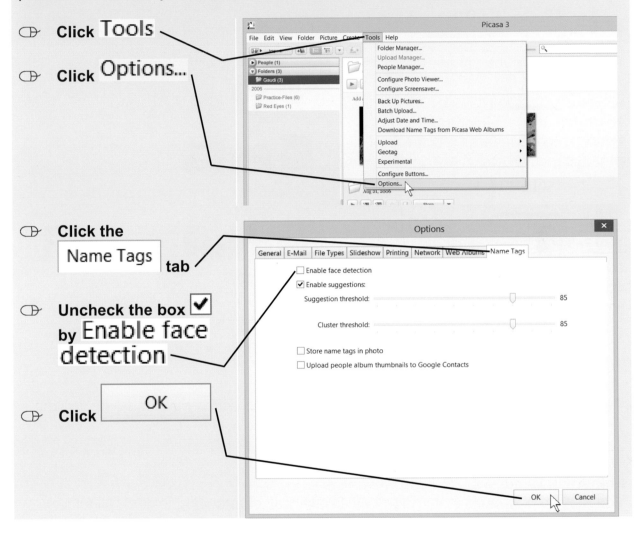

🔆 Tip

Screenshots

The screenshots you take of a full screen will directly be added to *Picasa*, below the Projects header:

⌨ **Briefly press** `PrtScn`

Please note: if you cannot find the `PrtScn` on your keyboard, then look for the button with the letters *PrtScn* and use this key together

with the `Shift` key.

You will see the screenshot appear below Projects in the ✳ **Screen Captures (1)** album:

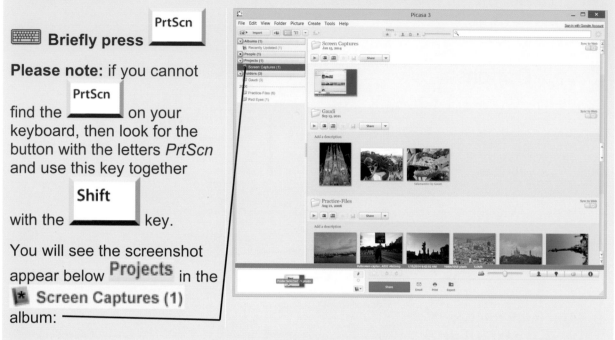

You can open this picture in *Picasa* by double-clicking it.

If you press both the `Ctrl` + `PrtScn` keys, the active window will be copied to the clipboard.

🔆 Tip

Folders in Windows

You may have noticed that *Picasa* has its own way of arranging folders. All folders are displayed one below the other. This order is different from the way in which *Windows* arranges the folders on your computer. You may find this awkward, because you will not be able to tell at a glance where a specific (sub) folder is located. If you do not like the *Picasa* folder layout, you can also select the *Windows* folder method. In *Picasa* it is called the *tree view*:

☞ **Click**

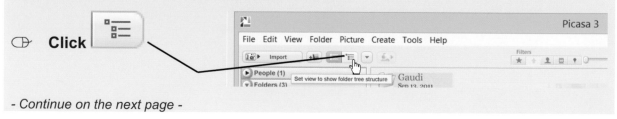

- Continue on the next page -

⊕ **If necessary, by**
Folders (7)**, click**

⊕ **If necessary, by**
Pictures (10)**, click**

⊕ **By**
Practice-Files (10)**,**

click ▷

Now the folders will be displayed in the same tree view as used in *Windows*:

You will see the folders with their subfolders below.

To go back to the *Picasa* folder layout:

⊕ **Click**

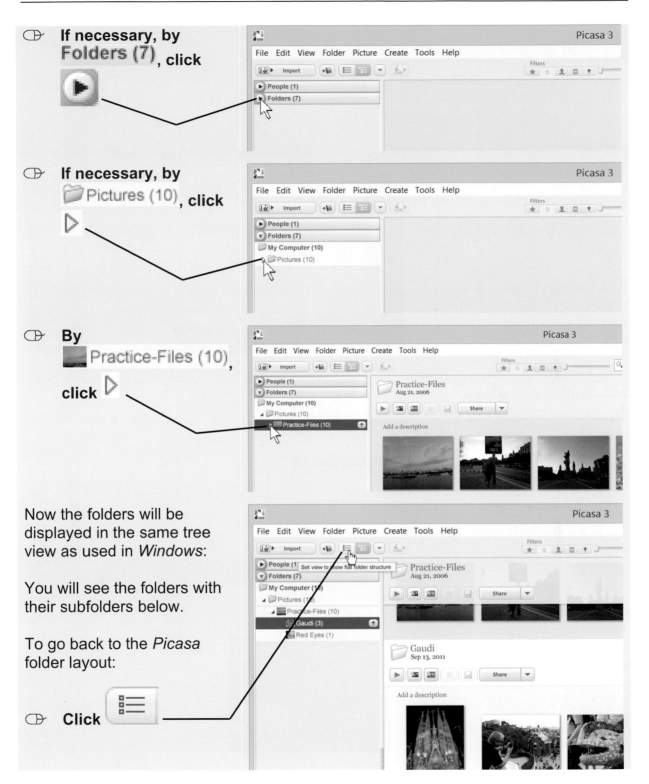

⚪ Tip

Disable the Picasa photo viewer

When *Picasa* is installed, the *Picasa photo viewer* will also be installed. The photos you open in *File Explorer,* whether it be from the desktop or other programs, will automatically be opened with the *Picasa photo viewer*.

Please note: In *Windows 8.1* you need to set *Picasa* as the default program for viewing photos.

☞ **Double-click a photo in *File Explorer***

The *Picasa photo viewer* will open:

The toolbar in the *Picasa photo viewer* window will appear when you move the mouse pointer downwards:

If you do not want to use the *Picasa photo viewer* you can disable it in *Picasa* like this:

☞ **Click** Tools

☞ **Click**
Configure Photo Viewe

☞ **Click the radio button**
⊙ **by**
Don't use Picasa Ph

☞ **Click**

Ok

Now your photos will be opened in your default program again.

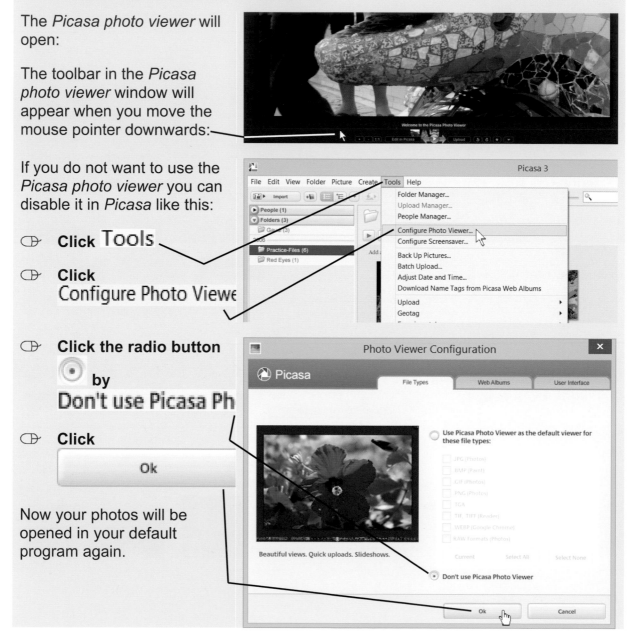

2. Editing Photos

In the old days you probably threw away a photo that had a bad exposure or displayed an object off kilter, but nowadays you can use photo editing programs such as *Picasa* to correct these faults. In many cases your corrections will be so successful that you can go ahead and print the photo or use it in a slideshow.

But not everything is possible: if a picture has been taken with a low resolution and you want to enlarge it, the results will be disappointing. A photo taken with a faulty exposure can sometimes be corrected, but the results would have been better if a proper exposure had been set up in the first place. It is a good idea to take the current lighting conditions into account before you begin snapping pictures.

Even some good pictures may still need a little correction from time to time. For instance, you may want to remove the red eyes caused by flash photography or adjust the overall color or contrast. *Picasa* provides automatic tools for correcting these things. You can also try applying a number of options manually one at a time.

You can use *Picasa* to rotate, straighten, crop and enhance your photos. By adding text or a special effect you can turn a simple snapshot into something really special.

In this chapter you will learn how to:

- correct photos automatically;
- correct the contrast;
- set the colors and correct the exposure;
- rotate and adjust the size of a photo;
- straighten a photo;
- correct red eye;
- add text to a photo;
- search for a photo;
- enhance and fine-tune a photo;
- coordinate the colors;
- use effects.

Please note:

In order to perform the exercises in this chapter you need to have downloaded the *Practice-Files* folder and saved it to the (*My*) *Pictures* folder on your computer. In *Chapter 1 Setting up Picasa* you can read how to do this.

2.1 Automatic Correction

Picasa provides several options to correct a photo automatically. Take a look at some of the options you can try:

☞ **Open *Picasa*** ✔️^{8}

☞ **If necessary, open the** 📁 Practice-Files (6) **folder** ✔️^{9}

👆 **Double-click**

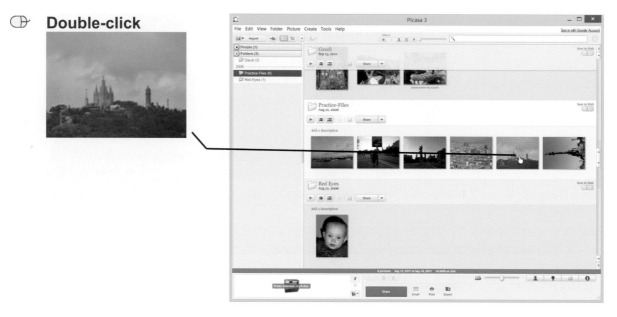

You will see the photo in the viewing pane:

The *Commonly needed fixes*

🔧 tab is already open:

This photo is dark, gloomy and rather hazy. You would probably not want to save it. But, take a look at what *Picasa* can do to improve it.

👆 **Click I'm Feeling Lucky**

The photo has become clearer and the colors are brighter. You will see much more detail:

The 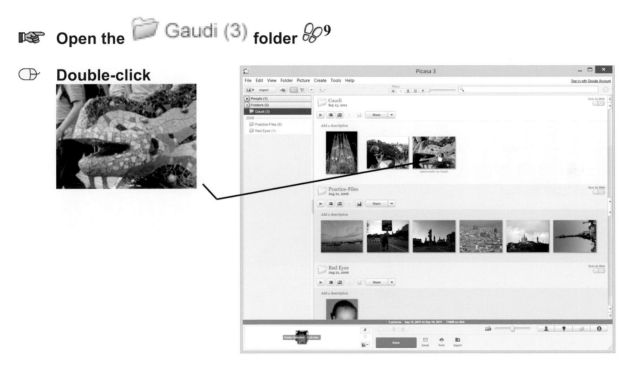 I'm Feeling Lucky button is no longer active. You can use this button just once for each photo: —————————

☞ **Go back to the *Library*** 🐾²⁰

☞ **Open the** 📁 Gaudi (3) **folder** 🐾⁹

⊕ **Double-click**

The *I'm Feeling Lucky* tool can also solve other small problems on photos that otherwise seem pretty good:

☞ **Click** I'm Feeling Lucky

The photo has become a bit more clearer and the colors have brightened somewhat:

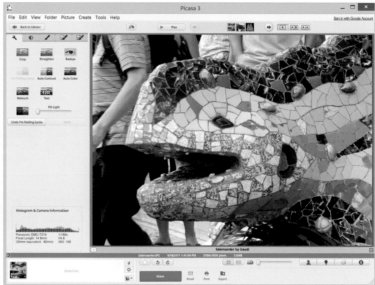

You can tell the difference a little easier, if you compare both versions of this photo side by side:

At the top of the window:

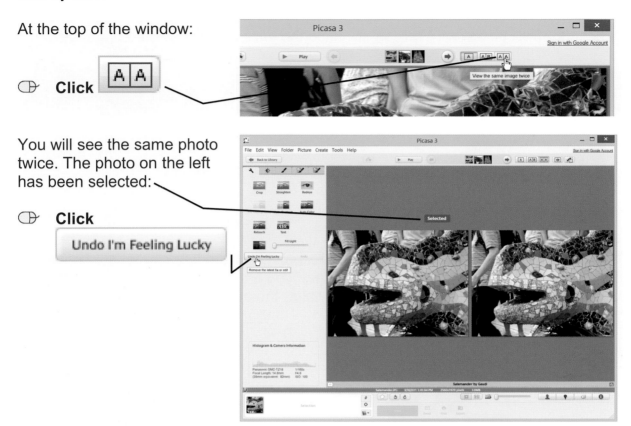

⊕ **Click**

You will see the same photo twice. The photo on the left has been selected:

⊕ **Click**

Undo I'm Feeling Lucky

The last edit on the left-hand photo has been undone. The photo on the right has been edited with the *I'm Feeling Lucky* tool.

You will see that the photo on the right is a bit brighter. You can save this version of the photo:

⊕ **Click the photo on the right**

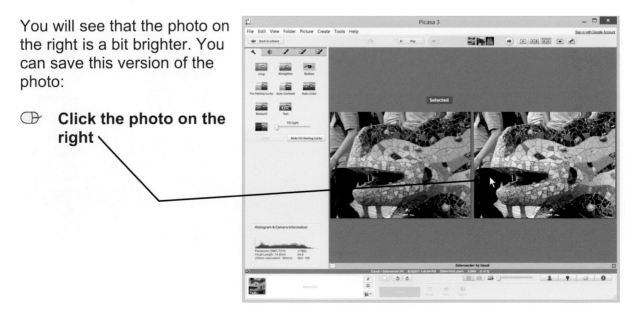

☞ **Go back to the** *Library* ✿²⁰

The version of the photo that is selected when you go back to the *Library* is the version that will be saved. You can still undo the edits on this selected photo by

using the | Undo I'm Feeling Lucky | button.

Any edits made on the photo that is not selected will be lost.

2.2 Correcting Contrast, Color and Exposure

When you use the I'm Feeling Lucky button, *Picasa* will attempt to correct the contrast, color and exposure of the photo, all at once. If you are not satisfied with the result, you can always correct the photo manually after the automatic correction:

☞ **Open the** 📂 Practice-Files (6) **folder** ✿⁹

☞ **Open the** **photo** ✿⁷

This photo has been taken at dusk. Since the sky behind the person is still quite light you will see some backlight.

⊕ **Click** I'm Feeling Lucky

The difference is hardly noticeable. See what happens, if you add some extra light yourself:

⊕   **Drag the slider** ⬚ **by Fill Light to the middle**

Now the details on the photo have become clearer:

![bandage icon] **HELP! I do not like the result.**

Have you edited the photo but are not happy with the result? Then click the

> **Undo I'm Feeling Lucky**   or   **Undo Fill Light**   button.
> The text you see on the button will depend on the last edit that was carried out.
> You can use this button to go several steps backwards and undo all previous edits.
> Even if you close *Picasa* and open the program again later on, you can still use this button. But once you have saved a photo this button will no longer be active. In *Chapter 3 Saving Photos* you will learn how to save a photo.

You can fill the light even more accurately, by using the slider. But the contrast and the color can only be corrected automatically. In *section 2.8 Fine-tuning* you will learn how to do this manually. Usually, both the contrast and the color will be

corrected by using the **I'm Feeling Lucky** button, but if you just want to correct one of these two elements you can use separate buttons. And in some cases you can also enhance the result of the auto-correct tool even further.

Go to the photo of the church on the hill:

⊕   **Click** ➡️ **three times**

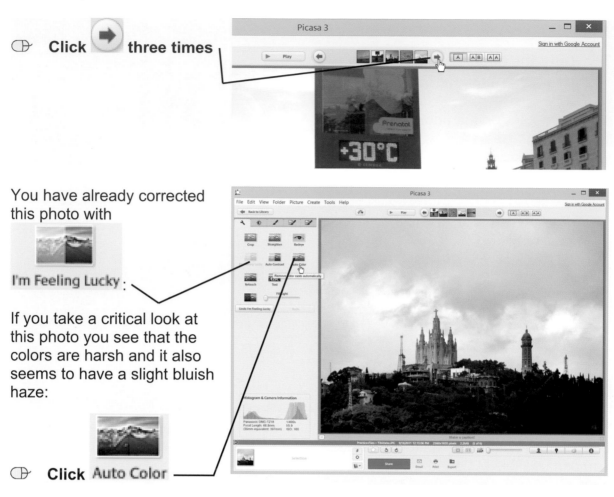

You have already corrected this photo with

I'm Feeling Lucky:

If you take a critical look at this photo you see that the colors are harsh and it also seems to have a slight bluish haze:

⊕   **Click** **Auto Color**

Now the sky has become grey, rather than blue-grey:

The photo appears to be a bit softer.

Of course, choosing the right color will depend on your own taste and the type of atmosphere you want the picture to reflect.

☞ **Go back to the previous photo in this folder** ✂21

You will see this pale, rather
hazy city view:

If the color of a photo is already pretty accurate, it is better not to use the

I'm Feeling Lucky tool. In such a case you only need to correct the exposure or the
contrast, for example:

⊕ **Click** Auto Contrast

The photo will gain more contrast and look less hazy:

2.3 Adjusting the Shape and Size

If you want to use a photo in a slideshow it should be positioned the same way as the other photos. This is how you rotate a photo:

☞ **Go forward, until you find the last photo in the folder** 👣²¹

At the bottom of the window:

🖱 **Click** 🔄

The photo has been rotated:

With 🔄 you can rotate the photo the other way round.

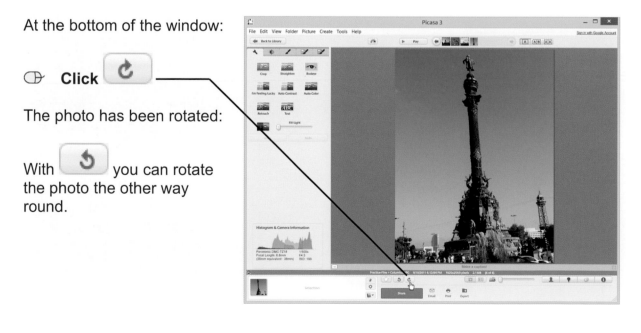

You will often see additional, unimportant items on photos or a few annoying details. Usually, these are things that nobody pays any attention to. For example, the signs, cars, and people at the base of the statue of Columbus. In *Picasa* you can remove these objects by cropping the photo:

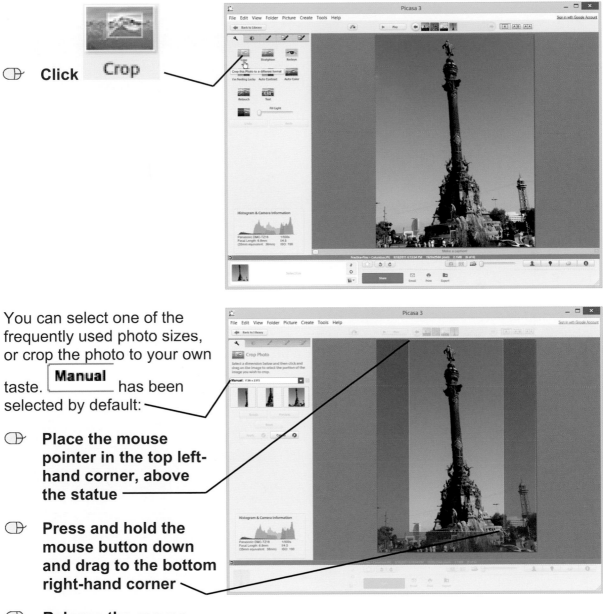

Click **Crop**

You can select one of the frequently used photo sizes, or crop the photo to your own taste. **Manual** has been selected by default:

- Place the mouse pointer in the top left-hand corner, above the statue

- Press and hold the mouse button down and drag to the bottom right-hand corner

- Release the mouse button

Please note:

Do not start too close to the statue's head but include as much of the sky as possible. In the next section you will see why this is important.

HELP! I cannot fit the statue in the frame properly.

If you do not like the result, click the ▢**Reset** button to try again.

👈 **Click**

▢**Preview**

You will briefly see what the cropped picture will look like:

Then the original picture will be shown once more.

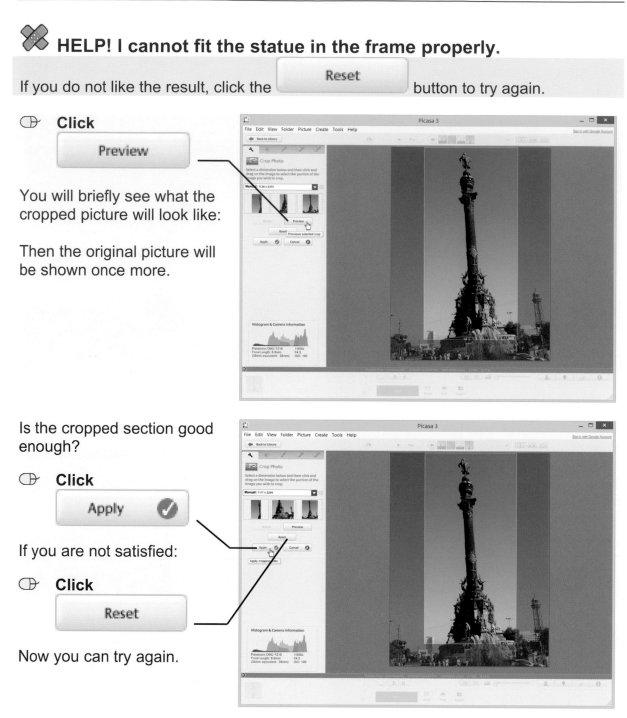

Is the cropped section good enough?

👈 **Click**

▢**Apply** ✅

If you are not satisfied:

👈 **Click**

▢**Reset**

Now you can try again.

You can also try to crop the photo to one of the standard sizes:

👉 **Go to the previous photo in the folder** 👣**21**

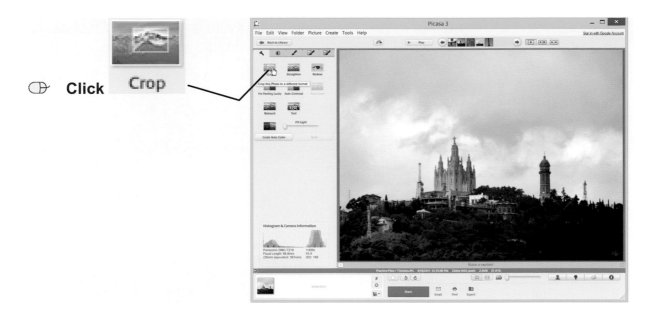

Click **Crop**

Select a 5 x 7 (10 x 15 cm) size for this photo. This is one of the regular sizes used by photo printing services:

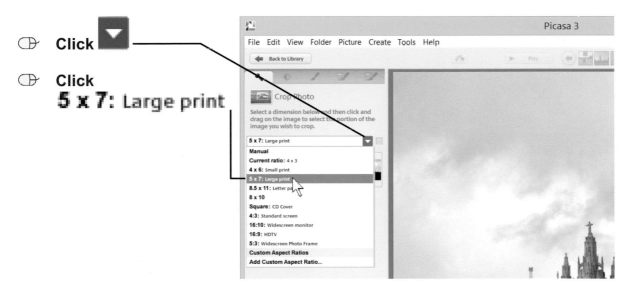

Click ▼

Click **5 x 7: Large print**

Picasa will show you three examples of cropped photos with a size of 5 x 7 inches (or 10 x 15 cm). Select the photo that comes closest to the image you want to use:

⊕ **Click the example on the left-hand side**

A frame appears on top of the photo:

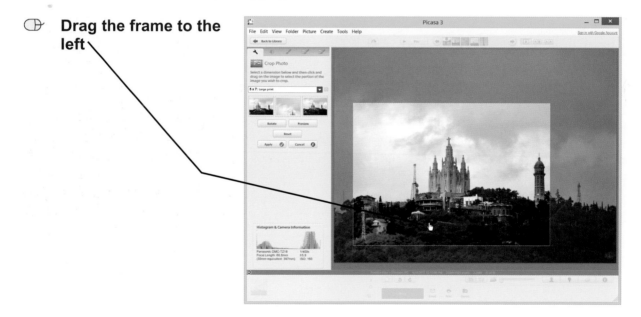

You can move this frame by dragging it:

⊕ **Drag the frame to the left**

You can also make the frame bigger or smaller.

⊕ **Place the mouse pointer in the top left-hand corner of the frame**

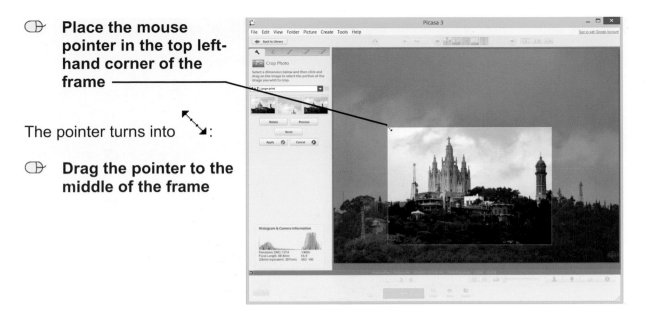

The pointer turns into ⤢ :

⊕ **Drag the pointer to the middle of the frame**

You will see that the frame becomes smaller but the 5 x 7 (or 10 x 15 cm) ratio is maintained.

This is how you rotate the frame:

⊕ **Click**

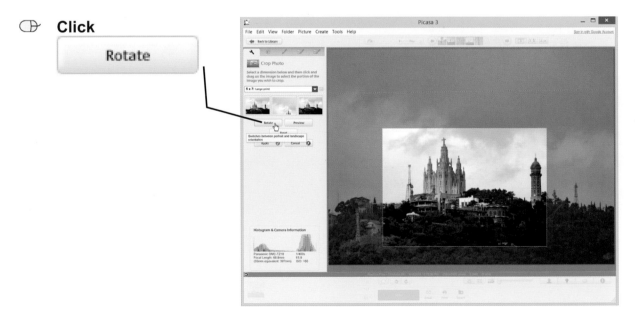

Now the aspect ratio of the frame is 7 x 5 inches (or 15 x 10 cm):

⊕ **Drag the frame to the**
    desired position

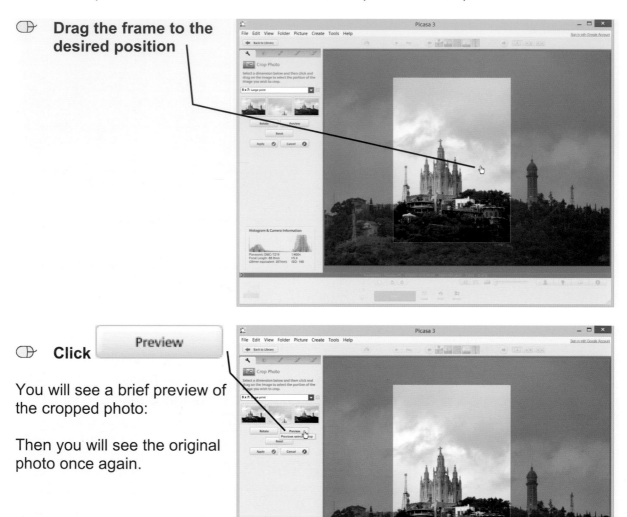

⊕ **Click** Preview

You will see a brief preview of
the cropped photo:

Then you will see the original
photo once again.

For now you do not need to crop the photo:

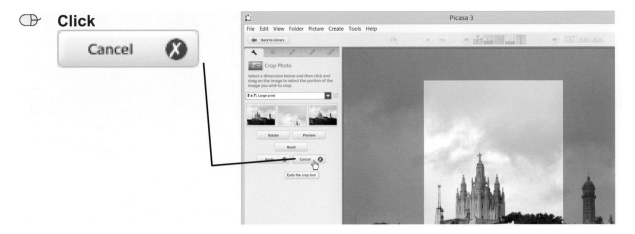

⌖ **Click**   Cancel ✖

The *Crop Photo* pane is closed and you will see the photo in the viewing pane again.

2.4 Straightening a Photo

You will often see objects a bit off kilter or notice that the horizon is a little tilted or slanted when you take pictures of buildings or scenery. You may have held the camera a little crooked or maybe you were standing on a slanted surface. You can use the *Straighten* tool in *Picasa* to improve these things:

☞ **Go back to the first photo in the folder** 👣²¹

You will see that the horizon is tilted in this picture of the harbor:

⌖ **Click** Straighten

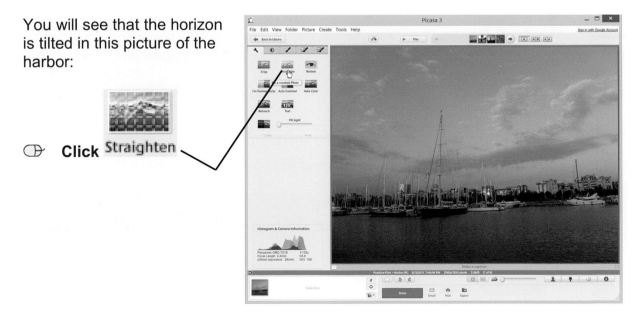

☞ **Drag the slider** ☐ **to the left a bit**

The grid lines will help you straighten the buildings.

If you are satisfied with the result:

☞ **Click** APPLY

If you are not satisfied, click CANCEL and try again.

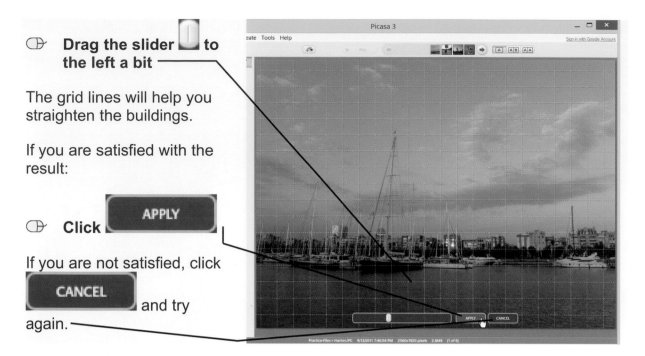

🩹 HELP! One of the borders of the photo has disappeared.
When the photo is straightened it will be rotated a little. The photo will no longer completely fill the selected size. *Picasa* will then zoom in a bit, and crop the photo on all sides, until the photo fills the selected size again. This will result in a slight loss of a part of the photo. Keep this in mind before using the *Straighten* tool.

💡 Tip
Straighten the center of the photo
Depending on your position and your camera lens, a photo may be distorted at the sides. Pay attention to the center of the photo as you try to straighten it.

You can try the *Straighten* tool again on the cropped photo of the Columbus statue:

👉 **Go forward, to the last photo in the folder** 👣²¹

You will notice that the tilting of the column is even more apparent once the photo was cropped:

☞ **Click** 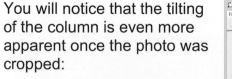 Straighten

👉 **Drag the slider** ▯ **to the left a bit**

👉 **Click** APPLY

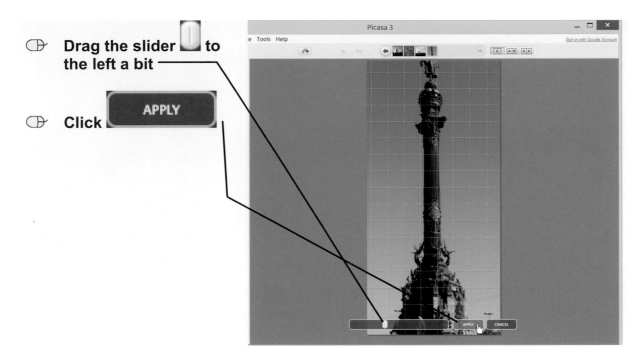

Although the column has been nicely straightened, something else has gone wrong. Since *Picasa* will zoom in on the photo a bit while straightening it, the borders have disappeared and so has the head of the statue. This was not actually the intention. Since you already selected as much of the sky as possible while you were cropping the photo, this problem cannot be solved. This is an example of a picture that was simply not taken correctly and unfortunately there is nothing more you can do to correct it.

The part of the photo that had been removed during the cropping action will still be stored in *Picasa*. If you decide to revert to the original, full picture, you will need to undo the straightening edit first.

👉 **Click**

Undo Straighten

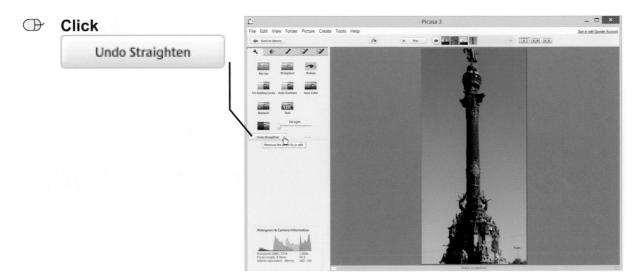

The column is tilted again and the statue is fully visible once more:

Now you can undo the cropping edit as well. First, click *Crop again*:

👉 **Click** Recrop

👉 **Click**

Reset

You will see the original photo:

👉 **Click**

Apply ✓

2.5 Correcting Red Eyes

When using flash photography you will often see that the people in the photo appear to have red eyes. *Picasa* has a special tool to help solve this problem.

☞ **Go back to the** *Library* 🐾[20]

💡 **Tip**
To the Library

By pressing [**Esc**] you will also return to the *Library*.

☞ **Open the** 📁 Red Eyes (1) **folder** 🐾[9]

☞ **Open the photo** 🐾[7]

🖱 **Click** Redeye

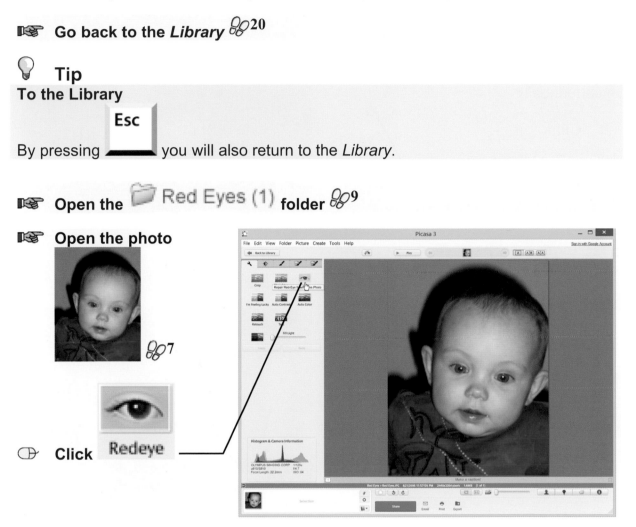

Picasa analyzes the photo and searches for red eyes. This may take a few seconds. Afterwards, both red eyes will be corrected:

You will see that both red eyes have been corrected:

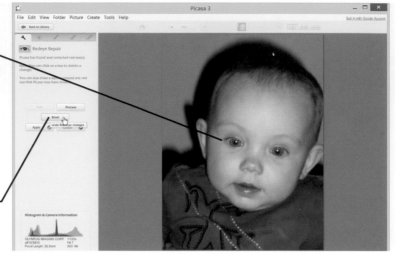

Sometimes *Picasa* will not be able to find the eyes. In such a case you can correct the eyes manually:

☞ **Click**

The red eyes are back again.

First, zoom in on the photo:

☞ **By** 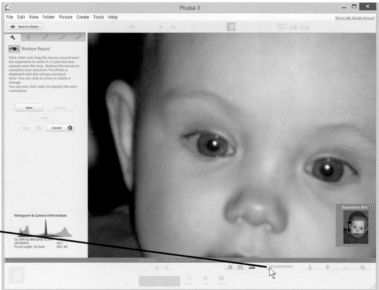**, drag the slider to the right a bit**

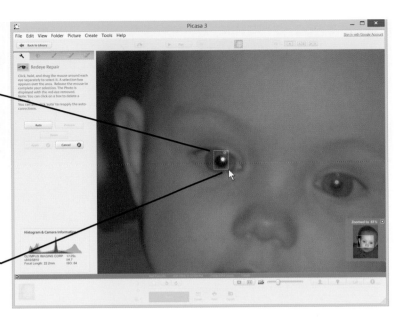

- ☝ **Place the mouse pointer at the top left of the red eye pupil**

- ☝ **Drag across the eye until the whole pupil is in the frame**

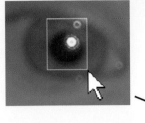

If you release the mouse button you will see the eye without the red pupil:

- ☞ **Correct the other eye in the same way**

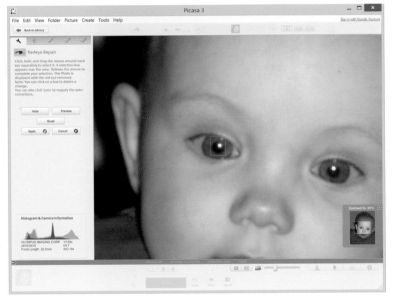

If you are you satisfied:

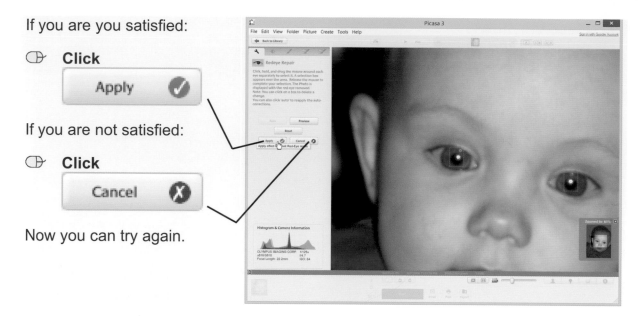

⊕   **Click**

If you are not satisfied:

⊕   **Click**

Now you can try again.

Adjust the photo in the viewing pane again:

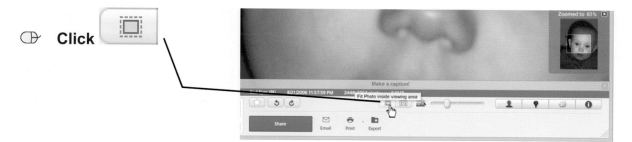

⊕   **Click**

You will see the full picture once more.

2.6 Adding Text to a Photo

If you add text to a photo, you can turn it into a kind of postcard.

☞ **Go back to the *Library*** ᵍᵍ²⁰

☞ **Open the**  **folder** ᵍᵍ⁹

☞ **Open the photo with the view of Barcelona** 𝒪𝒪7

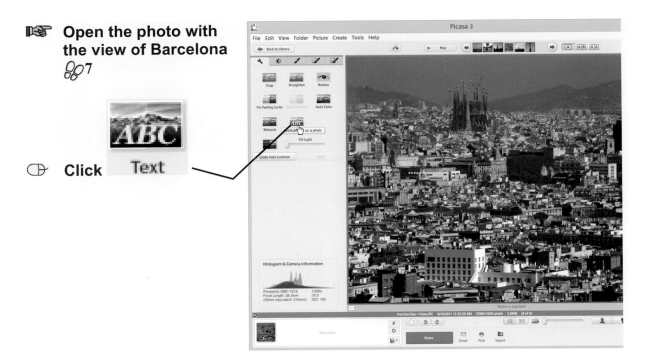

👆 **Click** Text

The text will be inserted on the spot where you place the mouse pointer. Position the text just below the center of the photo:

👆 **Click the photo**

⌨ **Type:** Greetings from Barcelona

The text is quite small. You can adjust the size like this:

⊕ By **Size: 12 ▼**, click **▼**

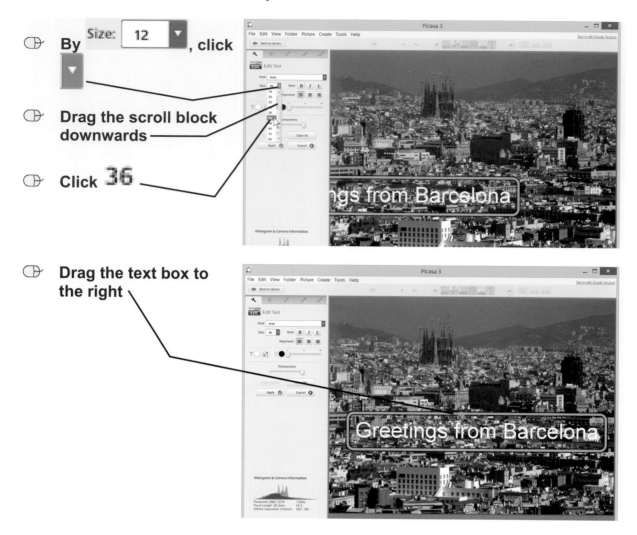

⊕ **Drag the scroll block downwards**

⊕ **Click 36**

⊕ **Drag the text box to the right**

The text will stand out more if you emphasize the letters by adding a border:

⊕ By **T ●**, drag the slider to the right

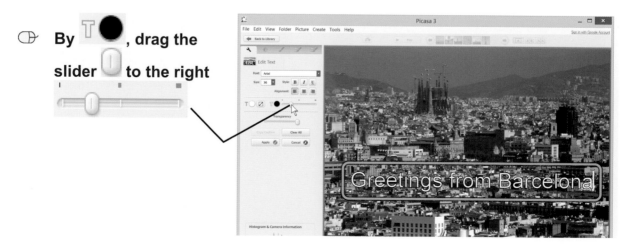

Color the letters:

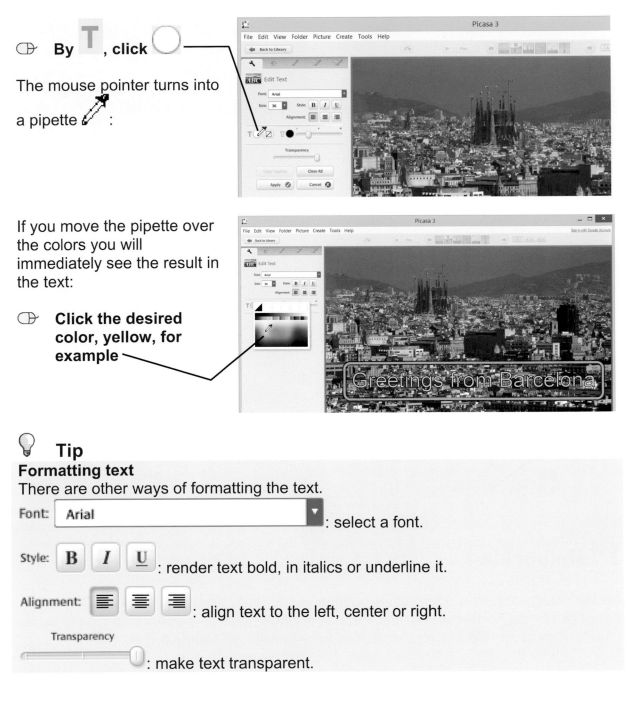

⊕ **By** T **, click** ◯

The mouse pointer turns into

a pipette 🖉 :

If you move the pipette over the colors you will immediately see the result in the text:

⊕ **Click the desired color, yellow, for example**

💡 **Tip**

Formatting text
There are other ways of formatting the text.

Font: **Arial** ▼ : select a font.

Style: **B** *I* U : render text bold, in italics or underline it.

Alignment: ≣ ≣ ≣ : align text to the left, center or right.

Transparency
⬤───────── : make text transparent.

Click

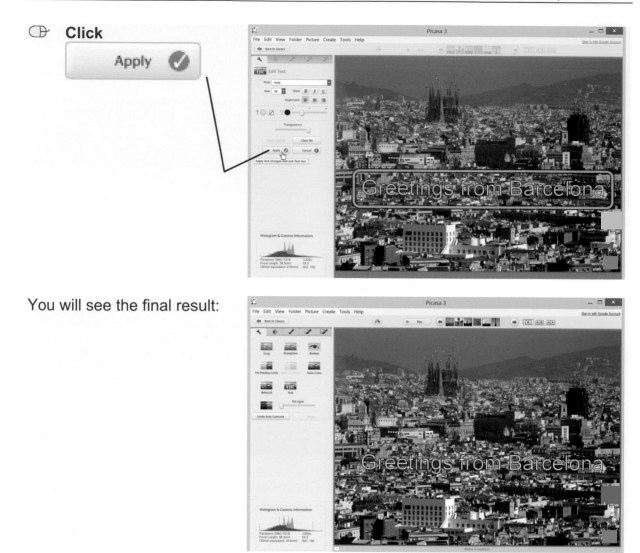

You will see the final result:

2.7 Retouching

A small irregularity can often ruin an otherwise perfectly good photo. Think of a hair or speck of dust on the lens, a crack in a scanned photo, or a disfiguring pimple on a cheek. *Picasa* can solve these problems for you with the *Retouch* tool.

☞ **Go back to the *Library*** 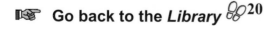[20]

Use the *Picasa* search box to look for a photo:

⊙ **Click the search box**

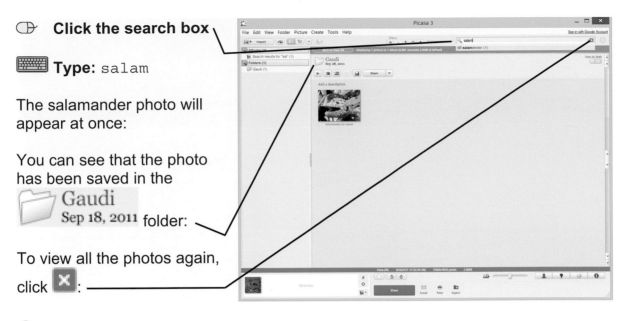

⌨ **Type:** `salam`

The salamander photo will appear at once:

You can see that the photo has been saved in the

📁 Gaudi
  Sep 18, 2011 folder:

To view all the photos again, click ❌ :

💡 **Tip**

Searching with Picasa
The *Picasa* search function searches for photo files, album names, titles, keywords and folder names that correspond with the word or expression that has been entered in the *Picasa* search box.

For example, if your computer contains a folder named *Photos of Mary* and also two photos in other folders, named *Mary at a party* and *John and Mary go fishing*, your search for 'Mary' will result in *Picasa* finding these two photos as well as all the photos in the folder named *Photos of Mary*.

☞ **Open the**  **photo** 🐾7

Zoom in on the photo:

☞ **Drag the slider by to the right**

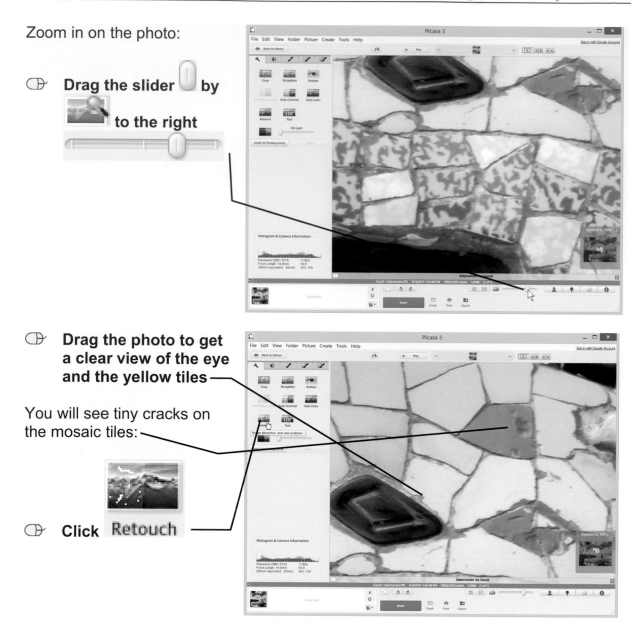

☞ **Drag the photo to get a clear view of the eye and the yellow tiles**

You will see tiny cracks on the mosaic tiles:

☞ **Click Retouch**

Retouching is a process that takes two steps. First you select the section of the photo you want to retouch:

☞ **Place the mouse pointer on the crack of the brown tile**

The crack is smaller than the circle of the mouse pointer. This circle is called the *brush*.

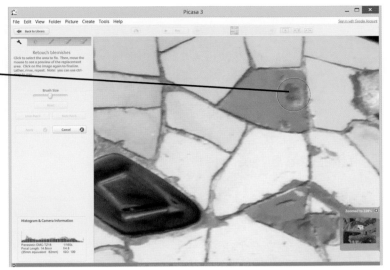

Adjust the size of the brush:

☞ **Drag the slider by Brush Size to the left**

☞ **Place the mouse pointer on the crack**

Now the crack will fit into the circle:

☞ **Click the crack**

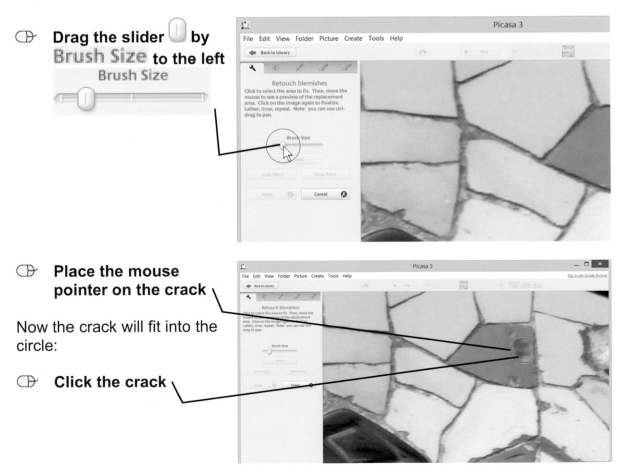

You have indicated which section of the photo you want to retouch. Now you need to select the section of the photo that will be used to replace the retouch area (the crack). You can use the undamaged part of the brown tile:

☞ **Move the pointer over the brown tile**

You will immediately see a preview of what the retouch area will look like:

☞ **Click the brown tile**

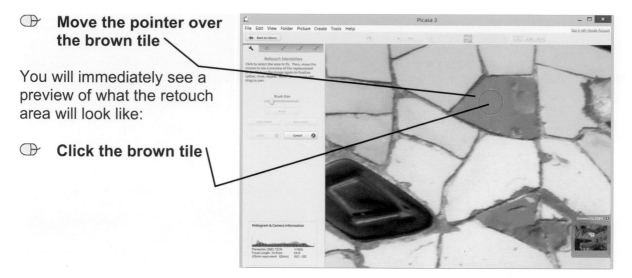

The result will not be perfect right away; you will still see the remains of the crack at the edges of the section. By retouching various parts of the crack, step by step, the full tile will be retouched in the final result:

☞ **Click the upper part of the crack**

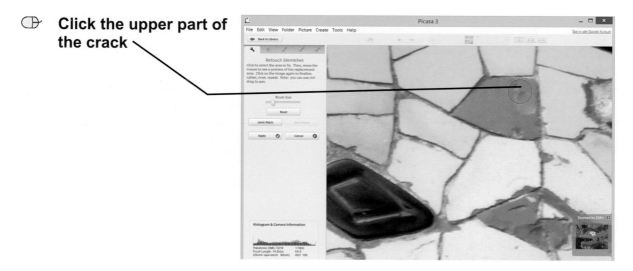

⊕ **Move the pointer over the brown tile**

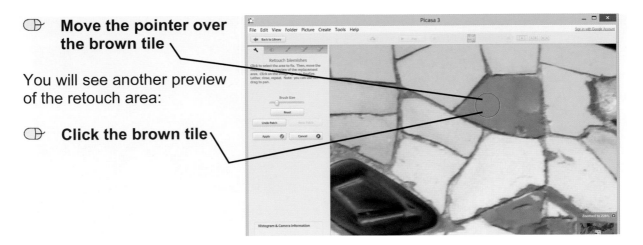

You will see another preview of the retouch area:

⊕ **Click the brown tile**

☞ **Repeat this action until all the cracks in the brown tile have vanished**

☞ **If necessary, enlarge the brush or make it smaller with**

before selecting the retouch area

💡 **Tip**

Not satisfied?

With the [Undo Patch] button you can undo the last patch.

With the [Reset] button you can undo all the patches.

With the [Cancel ✕] button you can undo all the patches and quit the *Retouch* option.

Eventually all the major cracks have been eliminated:

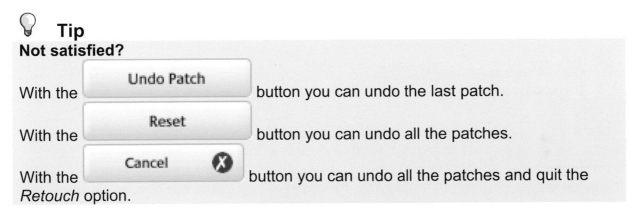

☞ **Adjust the size of the photo in the viewing pane** 👣**19**

You will see the end result:

If you are satisfied you can apply the corrections and close the *Retouch* pane:

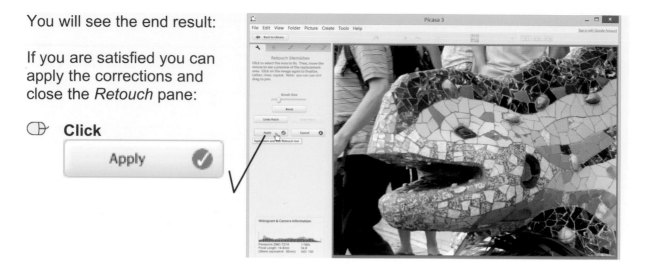

👉 **Click**

Apply ✓

☞ **Go back to the *Library*** 👣²⁰

With a bit of patience you can achieve good results with the *Retouch* tool. Not just with old or damaged photos, but also with sections of a photo you would rather not see. To obtain the best result, you will need to choose a replacement area that is close to the stain or crack on the photo. In this way the color and structure of the patch will match as close as possible to the area surrounding the original blemish.

2.8 Fine-tuning

Photos that have been taken in special lighting conditions, such as at the beach, in the snow, or at sunrise or sunset, tend to display unnatural colors. They will also sometimes have an incorrect exposure. If the automatic correction tools do not solve these problems you can try improving the photo using one of the options on the

Finely-tuned lighting and color fixes [⚙] tab.

👉 **If necessary, click [✕] by the search box**

☞ **Open the** 📁 Practice-Files (6) **folder** 👣⁹

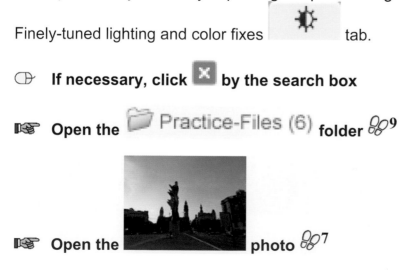

☞ **Open the** **photo** 👣⁷

This photo is too dark and has a shade of red because of the sunset:

⊕ **Click the** [icon] **tab**

You will see the fine-tuning options:

⊕ **Click** [icon]

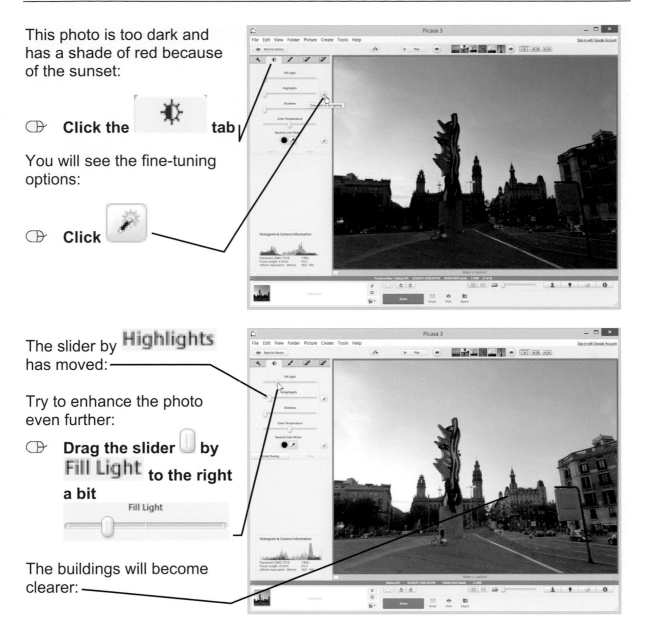

The slider by **Highlights** has moved:

Try to enhance the photo even further:

⊕ **Drag the slider** [icon] **by Fill Light to the right a bit**

The buildings will become clearer:

The *Fill light* option will lighten up dark areas, while the lighter areas will remain unchanged. With the *Highlights* option you can brighten the entire photo:

Drag the slider by **Highlights** to the right, like this

With the *Shadows* option you can make shadows even darker which will create more contrast and depth:

Drag the slider by **Shadows** to the right until you see

Now the photo will become a bit darker again.

You can lighten the dark areas of the photo a bit more:

☞ **Drag the slider by Fill Light to the right a bit**

The photo has become brighter and the contrast has improved. But you still see a redish hue. In the next section we will explain how you can correct this.

Which slider to use?
Use the overview below to decide which slider you should use to correct the photo in the best possible way:
- *Fill light*: to brighten a photo with backlight or a dark photo, and keep the detail in the lighter areas of the photo.
- *Highlights*: to brighten the entire photo, including the areas that are already quite bright. For the best results, you should use *Highlights* together with *Shadows*.
- *Shadows:* this will darken the shadows in the photo and in this way add more depth or contrast. Together with the *Highlights* slider you can enhance the contrast of a pale or washed-out photo.

You will often need to combine various options in order to achieve the best results.

The one-click fix button will help you apply the first corrections. This button works the same way as the *Auto Contrast* button on the tab, but here you can also adjust the effects yourself after having used this tool.

Source: Picasa Help

HELP! I do not like the result.

If you have applied a correction you do not like, you can click the

> **Undo Tuning**

button.

2.9 Coordinating Colors

By adjusting the color temperature you can make the photo appear *warmer* (redder) or *colder* (bluer). It's a good idea to display two versions of the same photo, side by side, before you try this option:

Click

Note that all the sliders have been reset to a position on the left of the bar:

This will not affect the edits that have already been applied to the photo.

The photo on the left has been selected, this is the photo you are going to edit:

☞ **Drag the slider by Color Temperature to the right**

The colors on the left photo will become redder, which makes the photo look 'warmer':

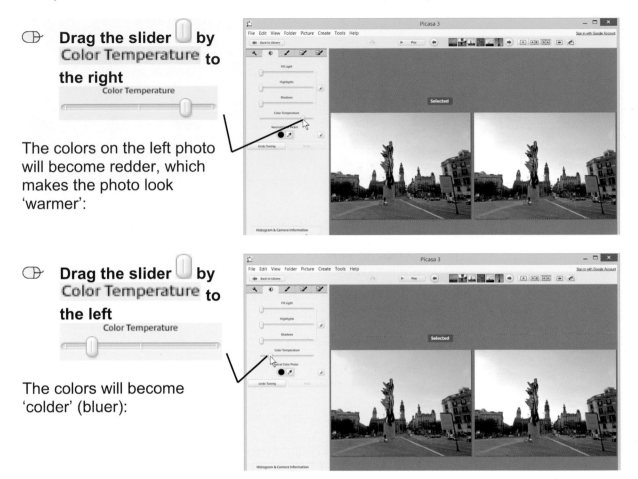

☞ **Drag the slider by Color Temperature to the left**

The colors will become 'colder' (bluer):

Of course, these corrections are far too extreme. Try to get a better correction:

☞ **Drag the slider by Color Temperature a bit to the right**

Now the photo looks quite nice:

You will see the difference with the photo on the right, where the colored hue is still visible:

☞ **Click**

Because a different edit has been applied to two versions of the same photo, you will be asked which of the two photos you want to save:

☞ **Click** Left

The edits you have applied to the left photo will be saved.

☞ **Open the**  **photo** 𝄎⁷

This photo has a yellow/orange glow because of the setting sun, especially around the buildings:

If a photo has a colored hue which does not display the white color of snow or clouds as true whites, you can try to solve this problem with the *Neutral color picker*. To clearly see the effects, first click a section of the photo that is not white:

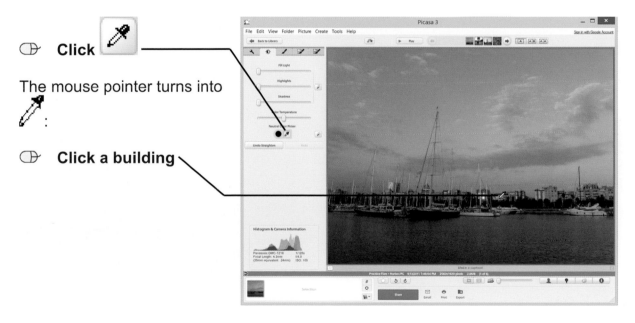

☞ **Click**

The mouse pointer turns into

:

☞ **Click a building**

The photo changes color:

The degree of discoloration depends on which area of the photo you clicked. *Picasa* will regard that spot as being white (which it was not, in this case) and will match the other colors accordingly.

⊕ **Click**

> Undo Straighten

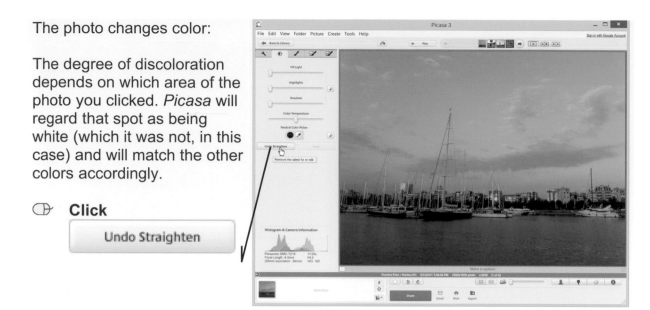

You will see the original colors again. The *Neutral color picker* will only work if you select an object that is actually white or grey. The other colors will be balanced on the basis of this object. Try now to select the white bow of one of the boats:

⊕ **Click** 🖉

The mouse pointer turns into
🖉 :

⊕ **Click the catamaran's bow**

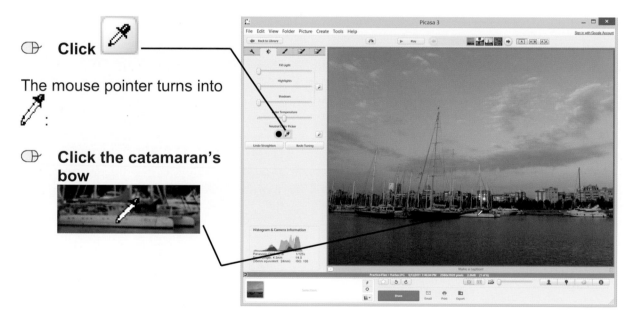

You will see the effect:

Adjusting the colors is not easy, and also depends on your own preferences. Do you want to create a warm picture, a clear photo, or a photo with lots of contrast? With *Picasa* you can edit the mood of almost every type of photo. Practicing with the various fine-tuning options will help you feel more comfortable using them.

2.10 Effects

You can also apply special effects to a photo. *Picasa* has three tabs with different effects. These tabs are called Fun and useful image processing , More fun and useful image processing and Even more fun and useful image processing . In this section you will be working with the options on these tabs.

☞ **Click the tab**

You will see various effects:

☞ **Click** Sharpen

If you look closely, you will see that the masts on the boats have become sharper:

This is how you intensify the effect:

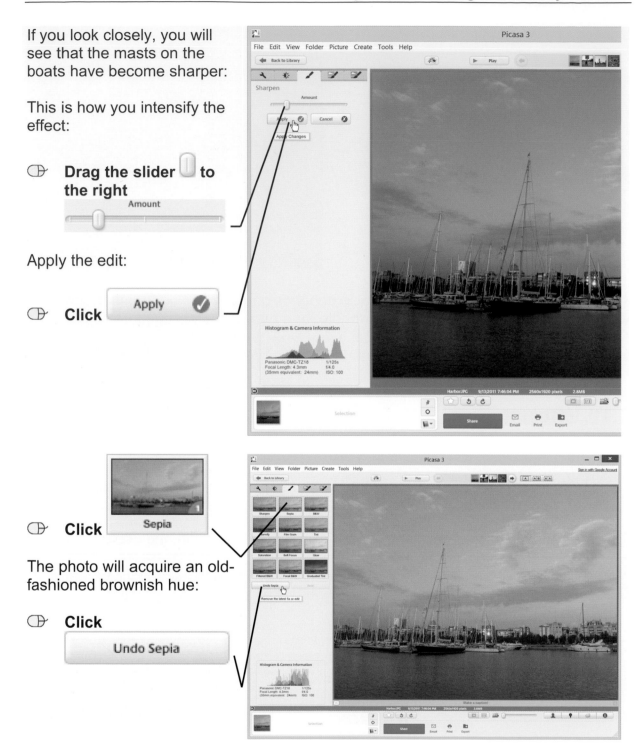

☞ **Drag the slider** ⎕ **to the right**

Apply the edit:

☞ **Click** Apply ✓

☞ **Click** Sepia

The photo will acquire an old-fashioned brownish hue:

☞ **Click**

Undo Sepia

Many effects will allow you to adjust the settings even further:

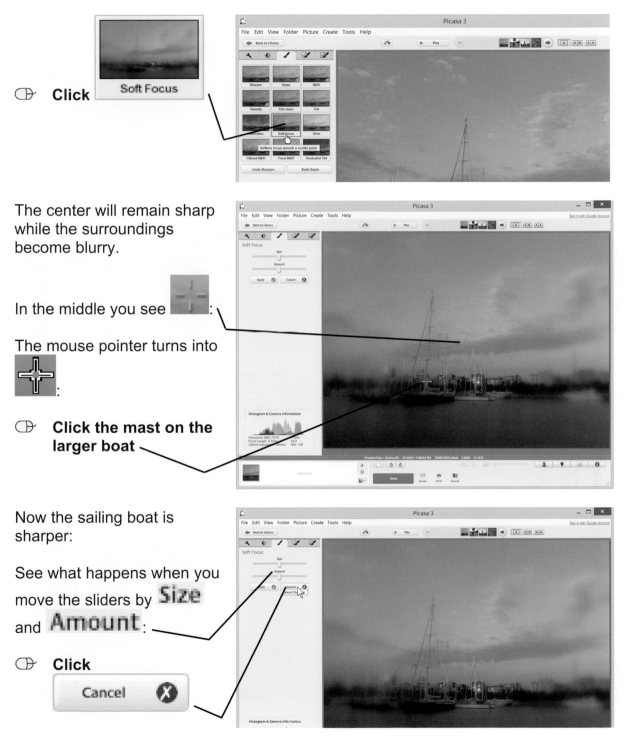

⊕ **Click** Soft Focus

The center will remain sharp while the surroundings become blurry.

In the middle you see ⊞ :

The mouse pointer turns into ✛ :

⊕ **Click the mast on the larger boat**

Now the sailing boat is sharper:

See what happens when you move the sliders by **Size** and **Amount**:

⊕ **Click** Cancel ✕

☞ **Go back to the *Library*** ⬬**20**

☞ **Open the**  Gaudi (3) **folder** ℰℰ9

☞ **Open the** [photo] **photo** ℰℰ7

Try another effect:

⊕ **Click** [Focal B&W]

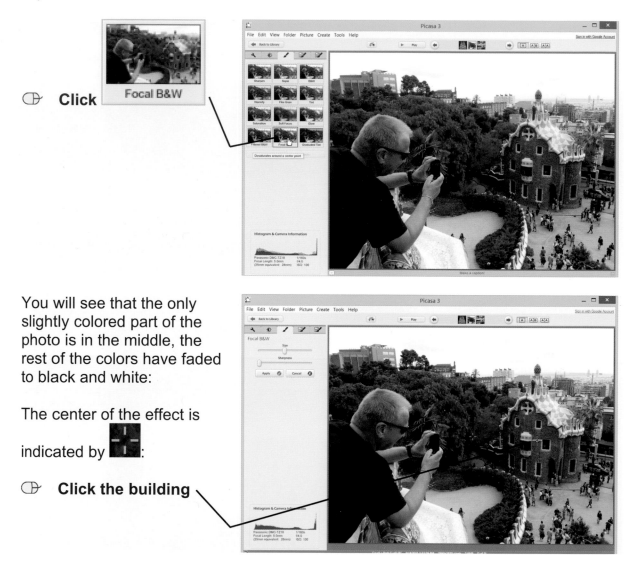

You will see that the only slightly colored part of the photo is in the middle, the rest of the colors have faded to black and white:

The center of the effect is

indicated by ✛:

⊕ **Click the building**

The building and the trees surrounding it still have a bit of color:

This is how you can brighten the colors and make the transition between the colored part and the black and white part sharper:

⊕ **Drag the slider** 🖱 **by** **Sharpness** **all the way to the right**

You will see the difference:

Make the colored section smaller and center it on the building:

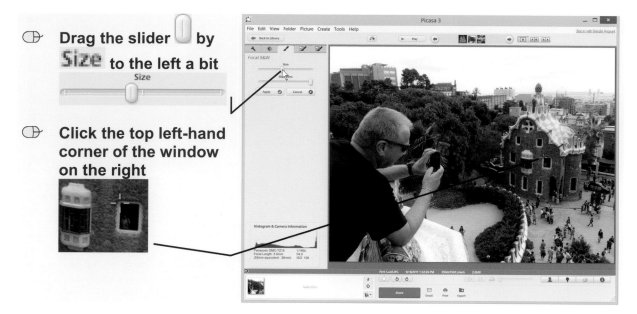

Drag the slider by Size to the left a bit

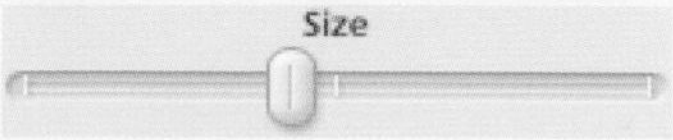

Click the top left-hand corner of the window on the right

This way you can emphasize a specific part of a photo.
You do not need to save this edit:

Click Cancel

Go back to the *Library* 20

Open the Practice-Files (6) **folder** 9

Open the  **photo** 7

◌➤ **Click the** tab

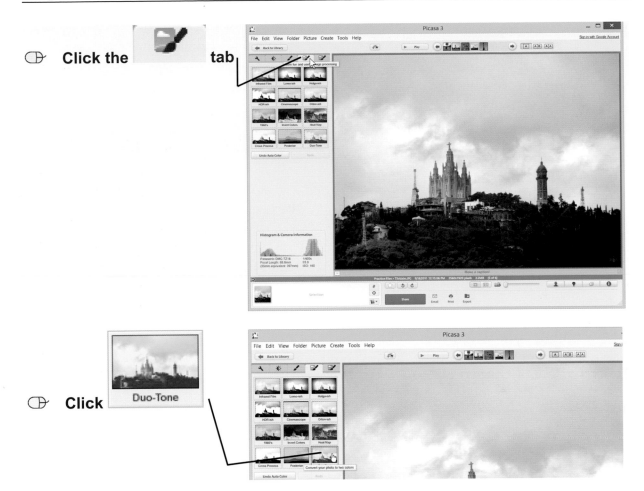

◌➤ **Click** Duo-Tone

The photo will be converted into a two-colored image. You can choose which colors are used:

◌➤ **By** Second Color,

click

If you move the mouse

pointer over the colors you will see the result in the photo right away:

⬚ **Click**

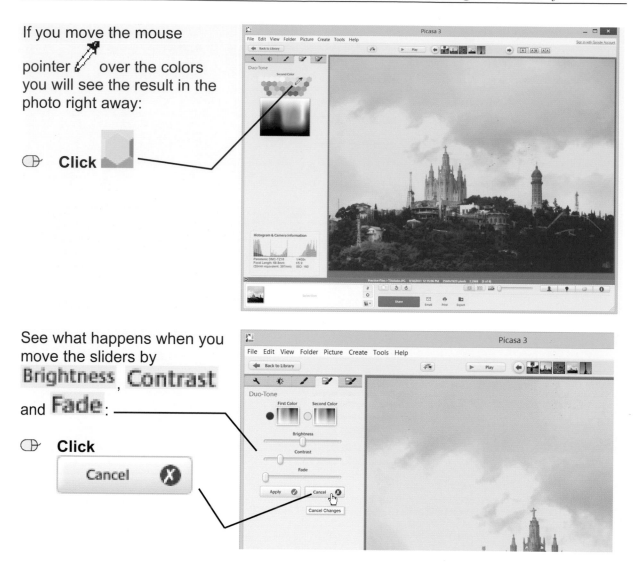

See what happens when you move the sliders by **Brightness**, **Contrast** and **Fade**:

⬚ **Click**

Cancel ✖

This is how you turn the photo into a picture taken in the sixties or seventies:

⬚ **Click** 1960's

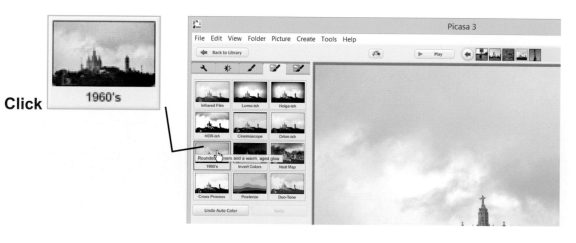

The photo now looks like a photo from an older photo album you may have in your own collection:

Older photos contain undeveloped silver in their emulsion, which causes a red discoloration after a couple of years.

☞ **Click** Cancel ⊗

You will see the normal colors again. The *Posterize* effect can be a very strange and alienating effect. Just try it:

☞ **Click** Posterize

The photo is hardly recognizable:

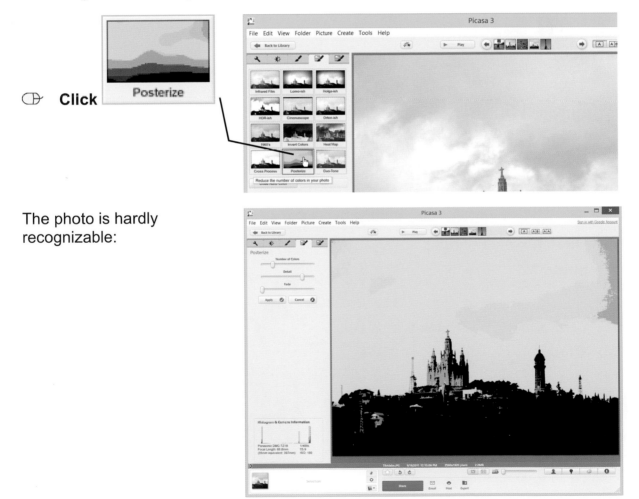

This effect will also let you adjust the settings yourself. This is how you add extra colors:

☞ **Drag the slider** ⬭ **by Number of Colors to the middle**

You will see that the photo has gotten more color:

See what happens when you move the sliders by **Detail** and **Fade**:

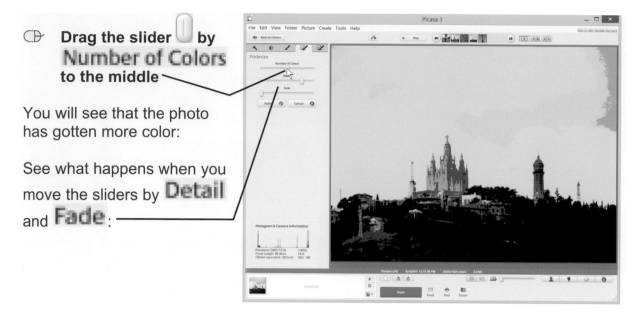

After you have finished experimenting:

☞ **Click** [Cancel ⊗]

☞ **Go back to the *Library*** 👣**20**

☞ **Open the** 📁 **Gaudi (3) folder** 👣**9**

☞ **Open the salamander photo** 👣**7**

☞ **Click the** [tab icon] **tab**

☞ **Click** [Pencil Sketch]

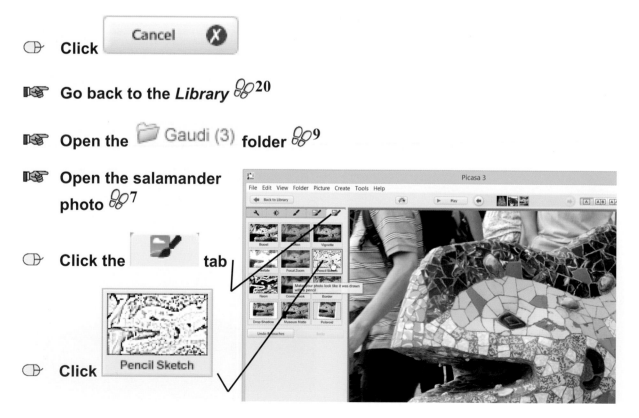

No the photo looks like it has been drawn by pencil:

⬚ **Drag the slider 🔘 by Strength to the right**

Strength

The effect will be intensified even further:

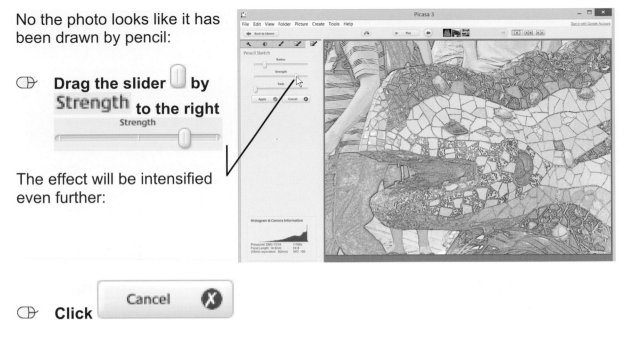

⬚ **Click** Cancel ✖

Try another effect:

⬚ **Click** Neon

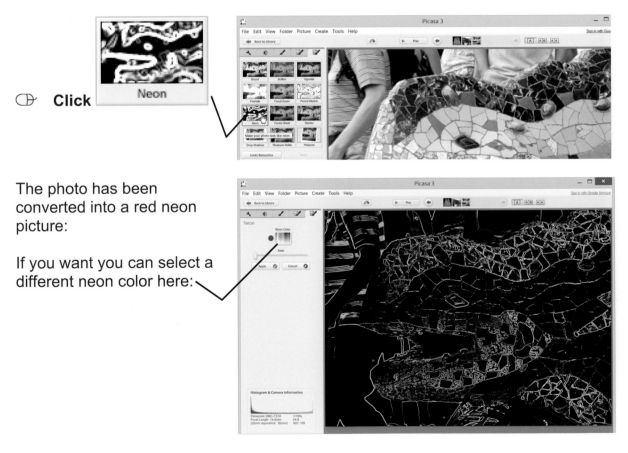

The photo has been converted into a red neon picture:

If you want you can select a different neon color here:

You can diminish the effect by fading:

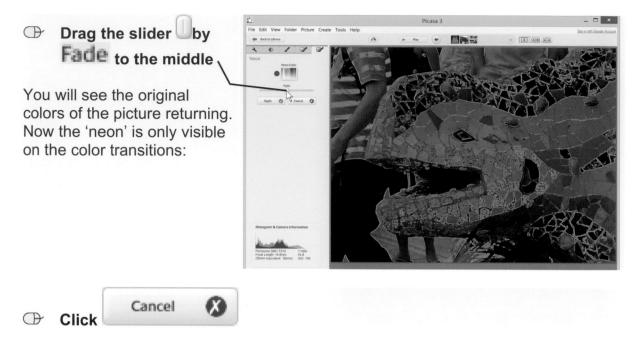

⊕ **Drag the slider** ⬜**by Fade to the middle**

You will see the original colors of the picture returning. Now the 'neon' is only visible on the color transitions:

⊕ **Click** Cancel ⊗

☞ **Go back to the** *Library* 👣[20]

By now you have gained quite a lot of basic knowledge regarding photo editing. In the next chapter you will learn more about saving edited photos.

☞ **Close** *Picasa* 👣[4]

2.11 Exercises

The following exercises will help you master what you have just learned. Have you forgotten how to do something? Use the number beside the footsteps 🐾[1] to look it up in the appendix *How Do I Do That Again?* The appendix is at the end of the book.

Exercise 1: Crop a Photo

In this exercise you will be cropping a photo to a size with a fixed aspect ratio.

☞ Open *Picasa*. 🐾[8]

☞ Open the *Practice-Files* folder. 🐾[9]

☞ Open the harbor photo. 🐾[7]

☞ If necessary, open the Commonly needed fixes 🔧 tab. 🐾[23]

☞ Open the *Crop* tool. 🐾[24]

☞ Select the fixed 3.5 x 5 inches (9 x 13 cm) ratio. 🐾[25]

☞ Select the left example of the cropped photo. 🐾[26]

☞ Rotate the frame. 🐾[27]

☞ Move the frame across the big sailing boat. 🐾[28]

☞ Make the frame smaller. 🐾[29]

☞ Move the frame so the larger sailing boat fits into the center of the frame. 🐾[28]

☞ View the example of the cropped photo. 🐾[30]

☞ Crop the photo. 🐾[31]

☞ Undo the cropping edit. 🐾[32]

☞ Go back to the *Library*. 𝄢20

☞ Close *Picasa*. 𝄢4

Exercise 2: Retouching

In this exercise you will be retouching one more section of the photo of Gaudi's salamander.

☞ Open *Picasa*. 𝄢8

☞ Open the *Gaudi* folder. 𝄢9

☞ Open the salamander photo. 𝄢7

☞ Zoom in on the yellow tile below the eye . 𝄢17

☞ If necessary, open the Commonly needed fixes tab . 𝄢23

☞ Open the *Retouch* tool. 𝄢33

☞ Select a smaller brush size. 𝄢34

☞ Retouch the irregularities on the yellow tile. 𝄢35

☞ Apply the corrections. 𝄢36

Exercise 3: Effects

In this exercise you will apply an effect to the retouched photo.

☞ Open the third effects 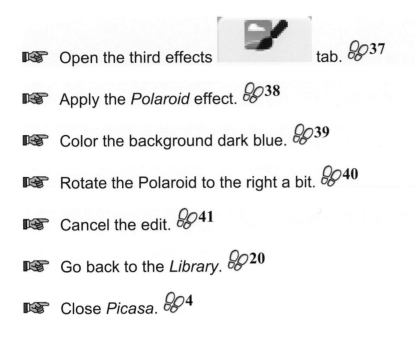 tab.   ℘℘**37**

☞ Apply the *Polaroid* effect.   ℘℘**38**

☞ Color the background dark blue.   ℘℘**39**

☞ Rotate the Polaroid to the right a bit.   ℘℘**40**

☞ Cancel the edit.   ℘℘**41**

☞ Go back to the *Library*.   ℘℘**20**

☞ Close *Picasa*.   ℘℘**4**

2.12 Background Information

Dictionary

Brightness	The amount of light that can be perceived in a photo. If the brightness is low the colors will fade, if the brightness is high they will become clearer.
Contrast	The difference in color between adjoining parts of a photo.
Crop	Cut off a portion of the photo you do not want to see.
Highlights	A method of filling in the light where the lighter parts will become extra light. It looks like they are highlighted.
Neutral color	The section of the photo that should be regarded as grey or white by *Picasa*. Then *Picasa* will match the surrounding colors on the basis of the selected color.
Pixel	The smallest element that makes up a digital image, also called dot.
Red eyes	The pupil of an eye reflects a red color. This may be visible on pictures taken with the use of a flash.
Resolution	The sharpness of a photo. The resolution is determined by the number of pixels the photo contains.
Retouching	Getting rid of ugly spots, scratches or other blemishes, in order to enhance the quality of a photo.
Sepia	A brown color that makes photos look old-fashioned.
Zooming	Enlarging (zooming in) part of a photo, or making it smaller (zooming out).

Source: Picasa Help

2.13 Tips

💡 **Tip**

View extra information about a photo
This is how you can view the settings used to take a picture:

☞ **Open the photo** 🐾7

You can see the information
on the left-hand side of the
window: ─────────

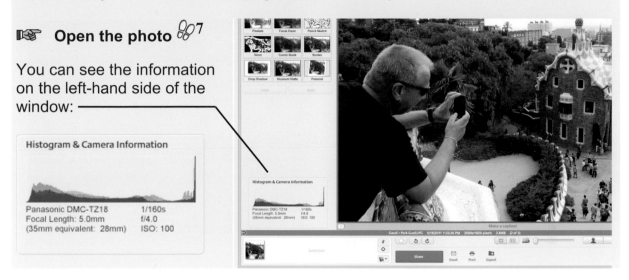

Histogram & Camera Information

Panasonic DMC-TZ18   1/160s
Focal Length: 5.0mm   f/4.0
(35mm equivalent: 28mm)   ISO: 100

💡 **Tip**

Editing multiple photos at once
This is how you edit multiple photos at once, in the same way:

☞ **Place the photos in the Photo Tray** 🐾22

⊕ **Click** Picture

⊕ **Click** Batch Edit

⊕ **Click the desired edit**

Now the edit is applied to all
the photos in the Photo Tray.
In this way you can enhance
a whole group of photos at
once.

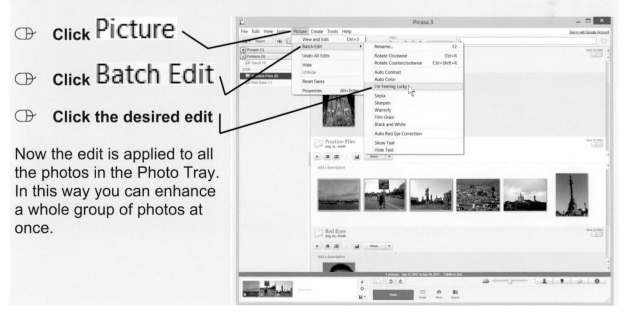

💡 Tip

Adjust the angle and scale of the text

Instead of displaying a text horizontally, you can also display the text on a photo slanted.

☞ **Move the mouse pointer across the center of the text box**

A circle appears

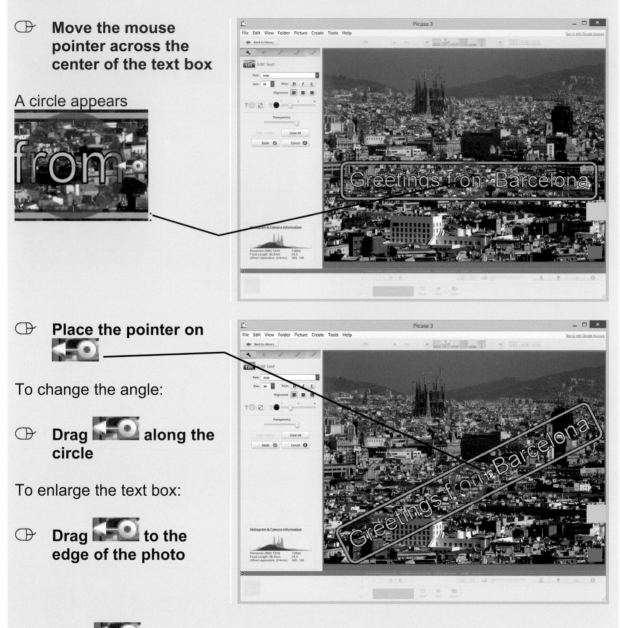

☞ **Place the pointer on**

To change the angle:

☞ **Drag along the circle**

To enlarge the text box:

☞ **Drag to the edge of the photo**

If you drag to the center of the circle, the photo will become smaller.

3. Saving Photos

In this chapter you will learn about the differences between various methods that can be used to save your edited photos. If you want to save your original photos without any edits, it is important to choose the right method when saving them.

You will also learn how to use *Picasa* to create a backup copy, and restore your photos from this copy. Saving a backup or safety copy is becoming ever more important, as nowadays many photos are only saved in digital form.

In this chapter you will learn how to:

- undo edits;
- save photos with the *Save* function;
- restore a photo to its original version with the *Revert* function;
- save photos with the *Save as* function;
- create a backup copy of your photos;
- restore the backup copy.

➥ Please note:

In order to perform the exercises in this chapter you need to have downloaded the *Practice-Files* folder and saved it to the (*My*) *Pictures* folder on your computer. In *Chapter 1 Setting up Picasa* you can read how to do this.

3.1 Undoing Edits

You have edited the photo named *Harbor.jpg*, but you have not yet saved it. Now you can undo all the edits, one by one:

☞ **Open *Picasa*** $\mathscr{O}\!\!\mathscr{O}^{8}$

☞ **Open the** 📁 Practice-Files (6) **folder** $\mathscr{O}\!\!\mathscr{O}^{9}$

☞ **Open the harbor photo** $\mathscr{O}\!\!\mathscr{O}^{7}$

⊖ **Click**

    Undo Sharpen

In this way you can undo every single edit, step by step:

⊖ **Click**

    Undo Tuning

You will see the
yellow/orange hue again:

⊖ **Click**

    Undo Straighten

Now you will see the original slanted photo, including the colored hue:

There are not any edits left to undo:

Picasa will always remember the edits you had already applied. This is how you apply the first edit once again:

⊕ **Click**

> Redo Straighten

⊕ **Click**

> Redo Tuning

⊕ **Click**

> Redo Sharpen

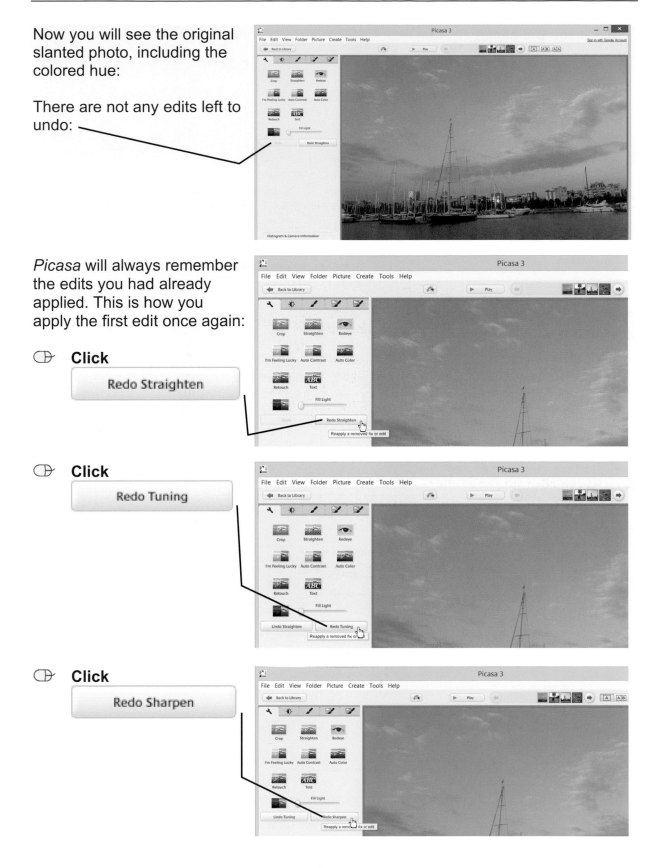

You will see the edited photo once again:

3.2 The Save Function

Saving a file in *Picasa* is different from saving a file in other programs, because *Picasa* remembers all the edits that have been applied to the file. That is why you can always restore your original version later on, if this is necessary. You can even do this after the file has been saved. You are going to try this with a photo to which you add an extra edit:

⊕ **Click the tab**

⊕ **Click** B&W

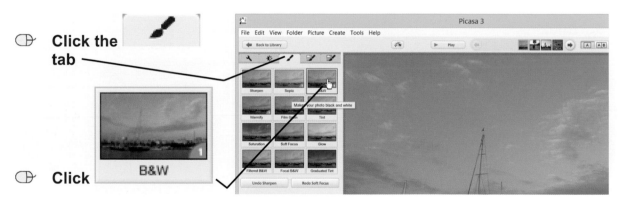

You will see the photo in black and white. Save the photo:

⊕ **Click File**

⊕ **Click Save**

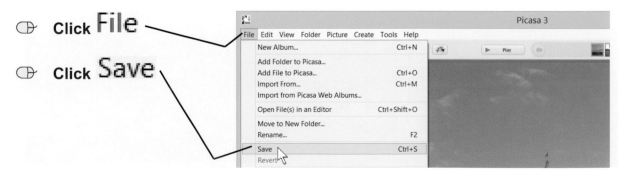

You will need to confirm this action:

⊕   **Click** | Save |

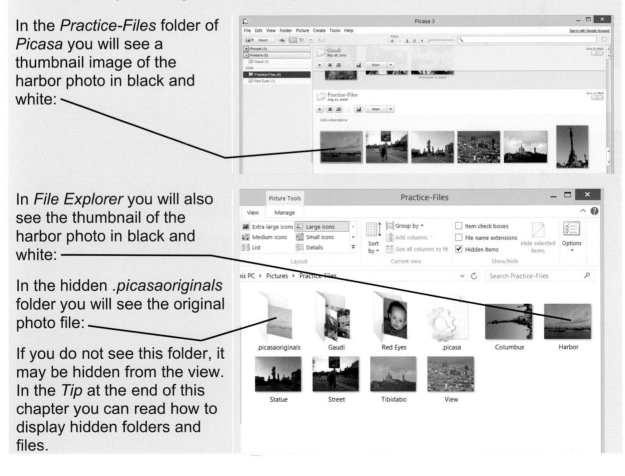

➦ Please note

The message A backup of this file will be made. does not mean that you will actually see an extra copy of this file in the *Practice-Files* folder on your computer. In *File Explorer* you will see that the edits have been saved in this file. But *Picasa* uses a hidden file to remember what the original file looked like. This file is stored in the folder named *.picasaoriginals* in *File Explorer*.

In the *Practice-Files* folder of *Picasa* you will see a thumbnail image of the harbor photo in black and white:

In *File Explorer* you will also see the thumbnail of the harbor photo in black and white:

In the hidden *.picasaoriginals* folder you will see the original photo file:

If you do not see this folder, it may be hidden from the view. In the *Tip* at the end of this chapter you can read how to display hidden folders and files.

Now you will see the

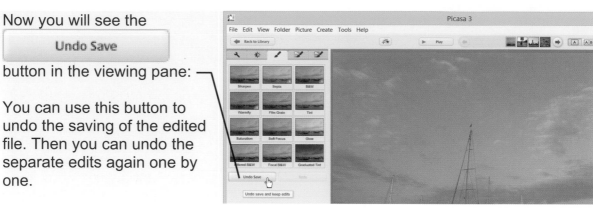

button in the viewing pane:

You can use this button to undo the saving of the edited file. Then you can undo the separate edits again one by one.

If you have used several tools and many different options to edit a photo it may take a while to undo all the edits one by one. It is easier to use the *Revert* function for this purpose. In the next section you can read how to use this function.

3.3 Reverting

An edited photo can be restored to its original version with the *Revert* function, which will undo all previous edits at once. This is how you use it:

☞ **Click** File

☞ **Click** Revert

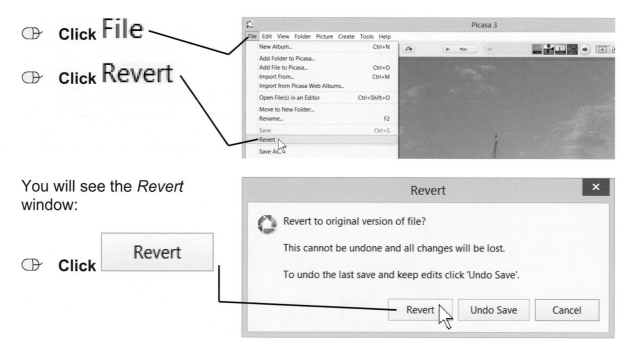

You will see the *Revert* window:

☞ **Click** Revert

If you want to save the changes you need to select | Undo Save |. Then you can go back and undo the edits in *Picasa* one by one, or use this version of the photo to apply new edits. Select | Revert | if you want to undo all the edits and go back to the original photo.

➥ Please note:

These functions will only work in *Picasa*. If you edit the photo in another program later on, the *Revert* function will not work.

You will see the original slanted photo again with the yellow/orange color:

Notice that the buttons for undoing and re-doing edits are no longer active:

☞ **Click**

Back to Library

Please note: it is possible that you do not see the original photo right away.

The thumbnail has already been adapted:

☞ **Double-click the photo**

If the settings weren't
reverted right away, you will
see the original photo now:

3.4 The Save As Function

In *Picasa* you can also select the *Save as* function. With this option you can save a copy of the edited photo with a different name.

☞ **Apply the *Sepia* effect** 🐾**38**

The effect has been applied
to the photo:

Save the edited photo:

Click **File**

Click **Save As...**

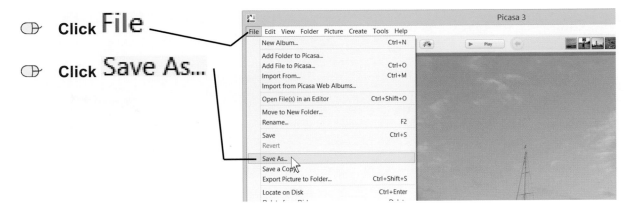

Enter an identifiable name for the photo:

The *Practice-Files* folder has already been selected:

Type: Harbor edited

Click **Save**

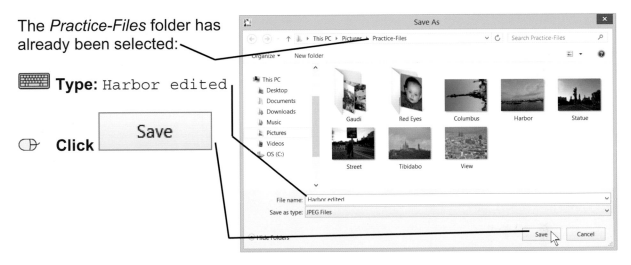

☞ **Go back to the *Library*** ✂20

Now the *Practice-Files* folder contains two identical photos:

Display the file names below the photos:

👆 **Click View**

👆 **Click Thumbnail Caption**

👆 **Click Filename**

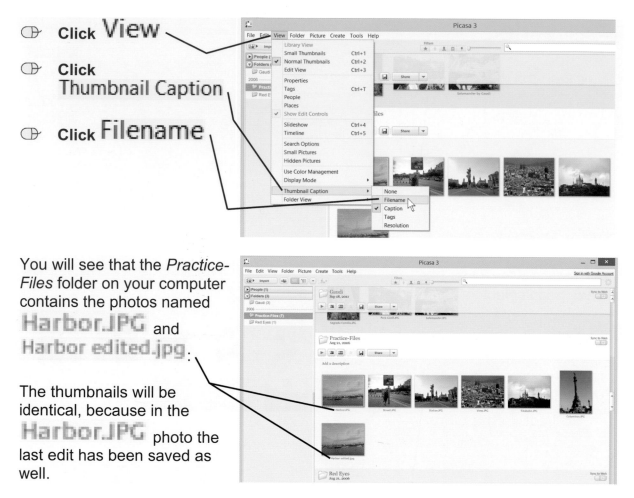

You will see that the *Practice-Files* folder on your computer contains the photos named **Harbor.JPG** and **Harbor edited.jpg**.

The thumbnails will be identical, because in the **Harbor.JPG** photo the last edit has been saved as well.

👉 **Open the photo named *Harbor edited.jpg*** 🐾⁷

The *Undo* and *Redo* buttons are not active:

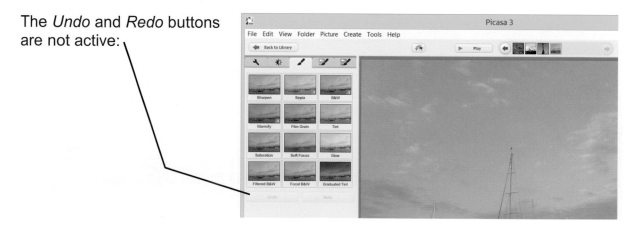

⬲ **Click** File

You will see that the
Revert option is not
enabled:

This means that once you
have saved an edited photo
with the *Save as* function, you
will not be able to revert back
to the original photo. But you
can still do this with the photo
named *Harbor.jpg*.

3.5 Creating a Backup Copy

It is important to create regular backups, especially if you save most of your photos
on your computer. A backup copy is a safety copy of your pictures. This is how you
create a backup copy in *Picasa*:

☞ **Go back to the** *Library* 🐾**20**

⬲ **Click** Tools

⬲ **Click**
Back Up Pictures...

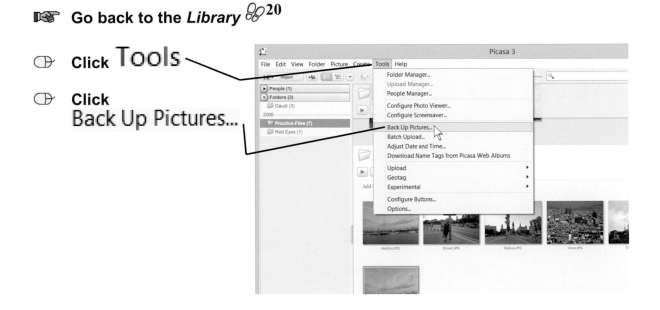

Backups are stored *sets*. The first time you do this, you will be creating a new set:

In the bottom left-hand corner of the window:

⊕ **Click** New Set

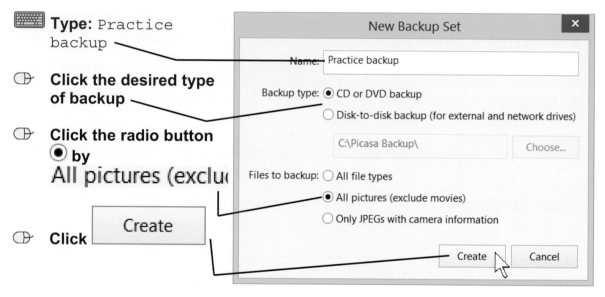

👉 Please note:

If you store the backup copy on your computer and nowhere else, you will not be able to use it, if your computer crashes or is stolen. That is why it is recommended to create an additional backup copy on a CD, DVD or an external hard drive.

⌨ **Type:** Practice backup

⊕ **Click the desired type of backup**

⊕ **Click the radio button** ⊙ **by** All pictures (exclu

⊕ **Click** Create

New Backup Set   ✕

Name: Practice backup

Backup type: ⊙ CD or DVD backup
⃝ Disk-to-disk backup (for external and network drives)
C:\Picasa Backup\   Choose...

Files to backup: ⃝ All file types
⊙ All pictures (exclude movies)
⃝ Only JPEGs with camera information

Create   Cancel

💡 Tip

Only your own pictures

If you only want to back up the photos you have taken yourself, and not all other kinds of pictures, such as icons or pictures you have downloaded from the Internet, you need to select this option: Only JPEGs with camera information. But keep in mind that the photos taken with your digital camera will have to be saved in the JPEG file format.

To the left of each folder you see an empty checkbox ☐:

☞ **Click**

Select All

☐ turns into ☑:

Or, if you want to select specific folders:

☞ **Check the box ☑ by these folders**

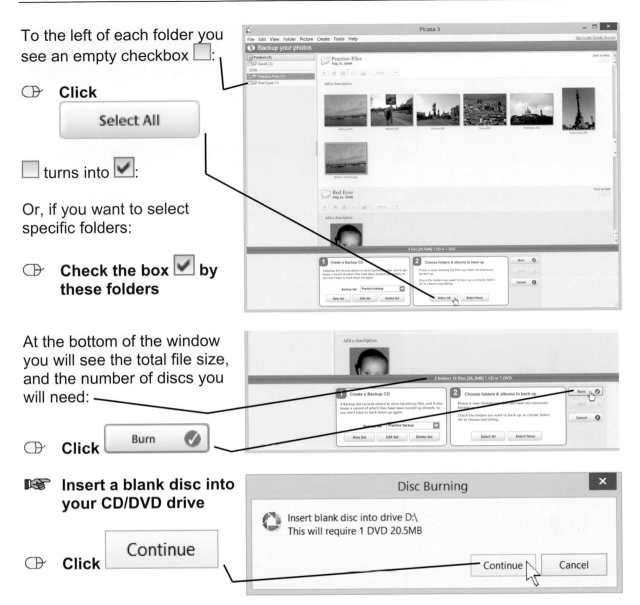

At the bottom of the window you will see the total file size, and the number of discs you will need: ——

☞ **Click** Burn ✔

☞ **Insert a blank disc into your CD/DVD drive**

☞ **Click** Continue

Instead of a blank disc you can also overwrite an older backup on a rewritable disc. You will receive a warning message first, to tell you that the disc will be overwritten.

On the right-hand side of this window you will see a progress bar:

Writing... 19.3MB of 30.3MB

After the disc has been burned:

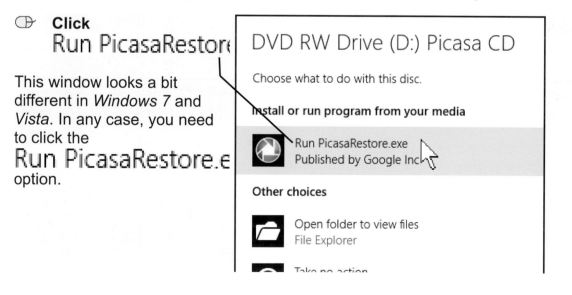

👉 **Click** ⬚ Eject CD

If you use a backup disc that you have created with *Picasa* and insert it into your CD/DVD drive, you will be asked whether you want to restore the files:

☞ **Insert the backup disc into the CD/DVD drive**

In *Windows 8.1*, on the desktop:

In the top right-hand corner:

👉 **Click**

In all *Windows* versions you will now see a window with various options for this disc:

👉 **Click**
Run PicasaRestore

This window looks a bit different in *Windows 7* and *Vista*. In any case, you need to click the
Run PicasaRestore.e
option.

If the photos need to be restored to their original folders:

👆 **Click** [Next]

If you want to restore the photos to a different folder, or a different disc, you need to click the radio button ⦿ by This folder:

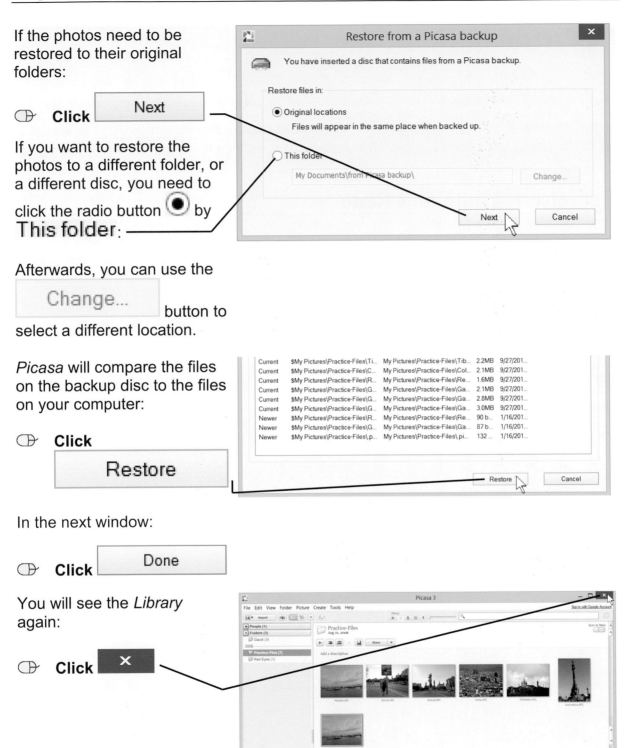

Afterwards, you can use the [Change...] button to select a different location.

Picasa will compare the files on the backup disc to the files on your computer:

👆 **Click** [Restore]

In the next window:

👆 **Click** [Done]

You will see the *Library* again:

👆 **Click** [×]

In this chapter you have learned how to save and restore a photo in different ways. You have also created a backup copy of your photos and restored it. In the next few exercises you can repeat these operations one more time.

3.6 Exercises

The following exercises will help you master what you have just learned. Have you forgotten how to do something? Use the number beside the footsteps 🐾[1] to look it up in the appendix *How Do I Do That Again?* The appendix is at the end of the book.

Exercise 1: Undo and Redo

In this exercise you will be applying a few edits, undoing them, and then redoing them again.

☞ Open *Picasa*. 🐾[8]

☞ Open the *Gaudi* folder. 🐾[9]

☞ Open the photo of the Sagrada Familia cathedral. 🐾[7]

☞ Open the first tab with effects [🖌]. 🐾[37]

☞ Apply the effects named *Sharpen*, *Tint* and *Soft Focus*. 🐾[38]

☞ Undo the edits one by one. 🐾[42]

☞ Apply the edits again, one by one. 🐾[43]

Exercise 2: Save and Revert

In this exercise you will be saving the photo you edited in Exercise 1. Afterwards you will revert the saved photo back to its original state.

☞ Save the edited cathedral photo. 🐾[44]

☞ Revert to the original photo. 🐾[45]

☞ Go back to the *Library*. 🐾[20]

☞ Close *Picasa*. 🐾[4]

3.7 Background Information

Woordenlijst

Backup copy   A safety copy of your files.

Revert   Putting back the files saved in a backup copy to your computer.

Source: Picasa Help

3.8 Tips

💡 **Tip**

Display the hidden subfolder named .picasaoriginals
By default, the *.picasaoriginals* subfolder will not be visible in *File Explorer*. This is how you can display it:

☞ **Open the desired folder in *File Explorer*, from within the *Picasa* program**
👣10

In *Windows 8.1*:

⊕ **Click the** View **tab**

⊕ **Click**

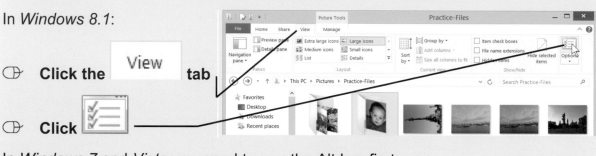

In *Windows 7* and *Vista* you need to use the Alt key first:

⌨ **Press** Alt

⊕ **Click** Tools, Folder options...

You will see the *Folder Options* window:

⊕ **Click the** View **tab**

Below Hidden files and folders:

⊕ **Click the radio button**
◉ **by**
Show hidden files,
folders, and drives

⊕ **Click** OK

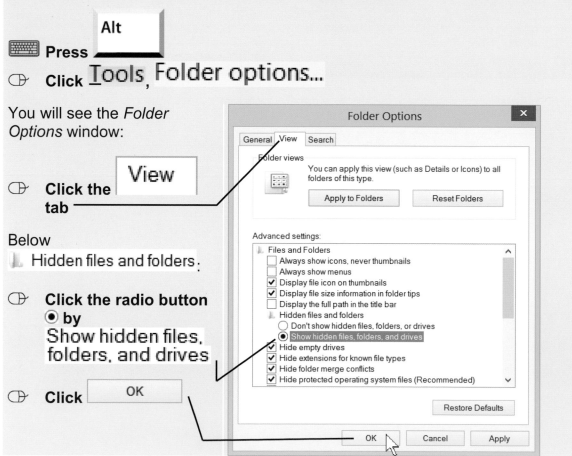

Tip

Export pictures
If you want to use another program to edit a photo that has already been edited in *Picasa* you will need to export this photo first. Then you will be able to edit the photo in the other program. Export the edited photos from the Photo Tray:

☞ **Place the edited photos that you want to export in the Photo Tray** 📖22

At the bottom of the window:

⊕ **Click** Export

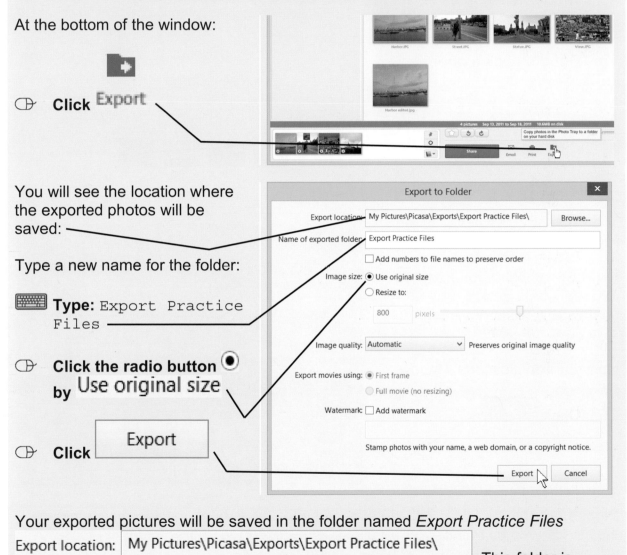

You will see the location where the exported photos will be saved:

Type a new name for the folder:

⌨ **Type:** Export Practice Files

⊕ **Click the radio button** ⦿ **by** Use original size

⊕ **Click** Export

Your exported pictures will be saved in the folder named *Export Practice Files*

Export location: My Pictures\Picasa\Exports\Export Practice Files\ . This folder is located in the (*My*) *Pictures* folder, in the *Exports* subfolder of the *Picasa* folder.

- Continue on the next page -

You will see a new window with a folder containing your exported photos:

☞ **Double-click the** **Export Practice Files** **folder**

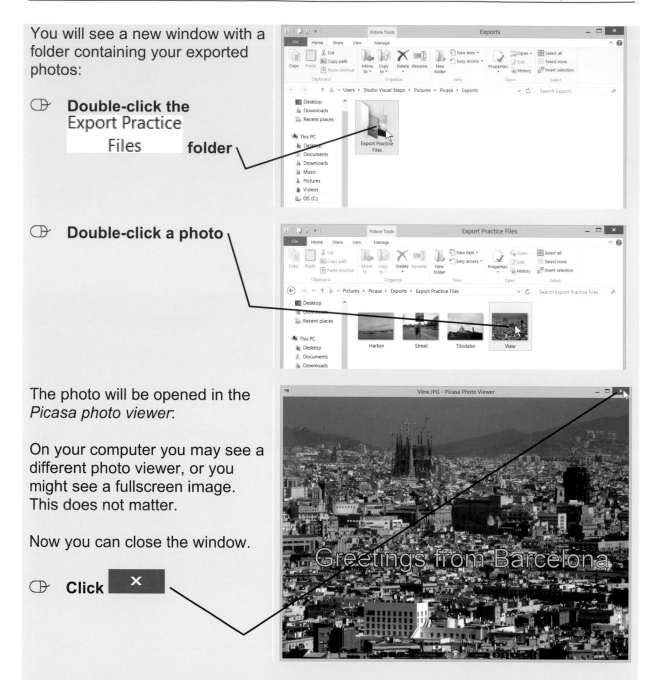

☞ **Double-click a photo**

The photo will be opened in the *Picasa photo viewer*:

On your computer you may see a different photo viewer, or you might see a fullscreen image. This does not matter.

Now you can close the window.

☞ **Click** ✕

Please note: if the folder with the exported photos has been saved within a folder that is scanned by *Picasa* you will also see this exported photos folder in *Picasa*. This will not happen in this example because you have set *Picasa* up to scan only the files and folders in the *Practice-Files* folder.

💡 Tip

Watermarks

You can protect your photos by adding a watermark to them. In *Picasa* a watermark consists of white text that is inserted into the bottom right-hand corner of a photo during the export operation. This is how you add a watermark to a photo during an export operation:

In the *Export to Folder* window:

☞ **Check the box ☑ by Add watermark**

⌨ **Type the text you want to display**

☞ **Click Export**

The watermark has been added to the photo:

💡 Tip

Save a copy of a photo

If you want to save multiple versions of the same photo you can save a copy of the photo:

☞ **Click the photo**

☞ **Click** File

☞ **Click** Save a Copy

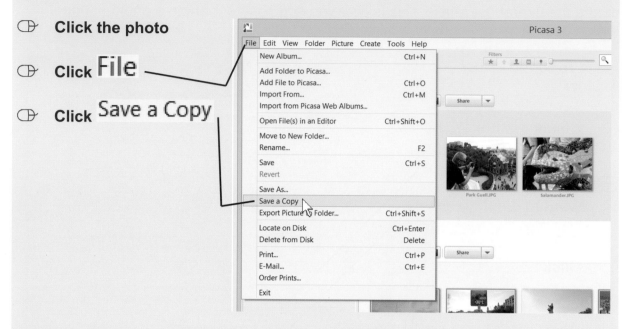

A copy of this photo will be saved, in the same folder as the original photo. The file name of the copy is the same as the name of the original photo, but with an extra digit: -001. For example, the copy of the photo named S*treet.jpg* is named *Street-001.jpg*.

4. Fun and Useful Extras in Picasa

Picasa has some nice extra features. Such as the option to create a collage or view a slideshow of your photos.

If you have a large number of photos that you would like to share with other people, you might consider making a gift CD. You can create a CD by burning a regular slideshow of the photos you have selected to the CD. This CD or DVD can be played on another computer and on most DVD players as well.

Another great option is making a video of a slideshow. You can select which transitions you want to use between the slides, and the time period for the slides to be displayed. You can also add music to your video. After you have finished the video you can even upload it to *YouTube*, if you want.

In this chapter you will learn how to:

- create collages;
- view photos in a slideshow;
- create a gift CD;
- turn a slideshow into a video;
- add and edit a title slide;
- set transitions;
- add music;
- save a video;
- crop video clips;
- add video clips to a video;
- upload a video to *YouTube*;
- use photos as a screensaver or wallpaper for your desktop.

➥ Please note:

In order to perform the exercises in this chapter you need to have downloaded the *Practice-Files* folder and saved it to the (*My*) *Pictures* folder on your computer. In *Chapter 1 Setting up Picasa* you can read how to do this.

4.1 Creating a Collage

Creating a collage is a fun way of displaying multiple photos on a single page in a playful way. You can choose from several different styles for your collage.

☞ **Place five photos in the Photo Tray** 👣²²

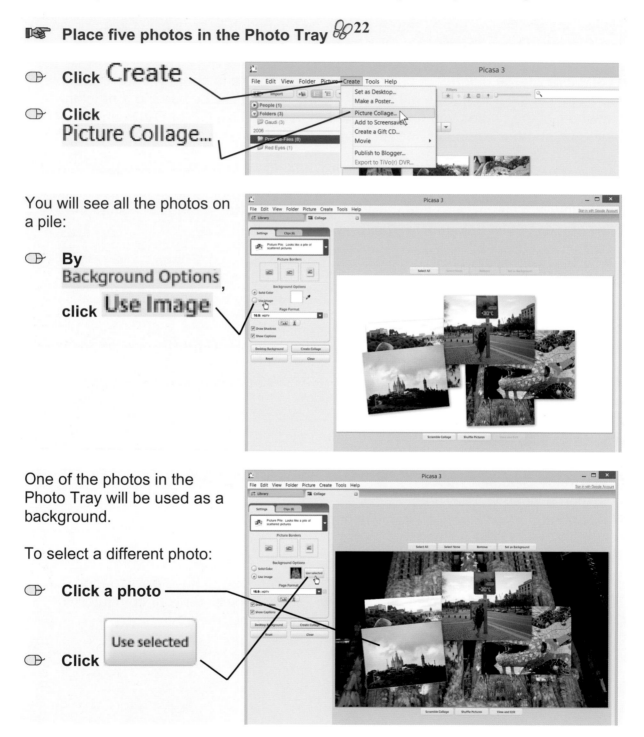

☞ Click **Create**

☞ Click
Picture Collage...

You will see all the photos on a pile:

☞ **By**
Background Options,
click **Use Image**

One of the photos in the Photo Tray will be used as a background.

To select a different photo:

☞ **Click a photo**

☞ **Click** Use selected

The layout of the collage has not been fixed yet. You can drag the photos to a different position:

☞ **Drag the photos to the desired location**

Some of the photos are slightly tilted. This is how you determine the angle of the tilt and size of the images that are displayed:

⊕ **Click a photo**

⊕ **Place the mouse pointer on**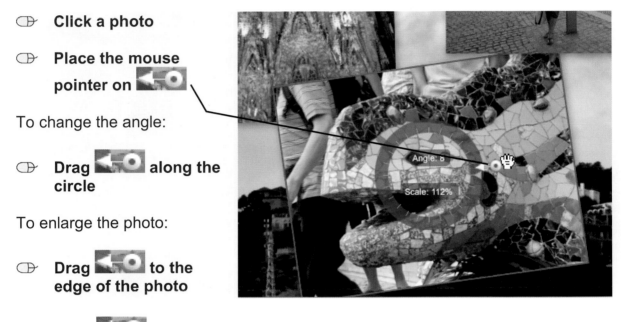

To change the angle:

⊕ **Drag** along the circle

To enlarge the photo:

⊕ **Drag** to the edge of the photo

If you drag to the middle of the circle, the photo will become smaller.

This is how you add a border to the photos:

⊕ **Click the background photo**

⊕ **By** Picture Borders, click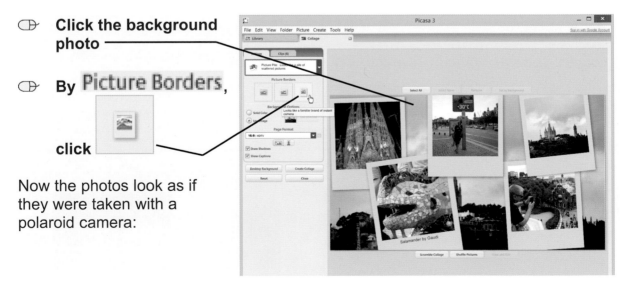

Now the photos look as if they were taken with a polaroid camera:

You can also select a different layout:

⊕ **By**

Picture Pile: Looks like a pile of scattered pictures

,

click

⊕ **Click**

Mosaic: Automaticall
page

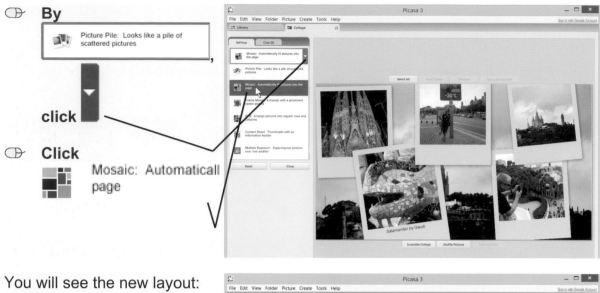

You will see the new layout:

This is how can widen the space between the photos:

⊕ **Drag the slider ▯ by Grid Spacing to the right**

None   Max.

If you are satisfied you can save the end result as a collage:

⊕ **Click**

Create Collage

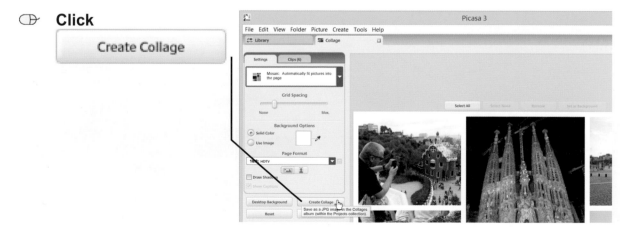

The collage will be created.

You will see the collage in the viewing pane:

You can edit and print this collage in the same way as a regular photo. In *Chapter 6 Printing Photos* you can read how to print a photo.

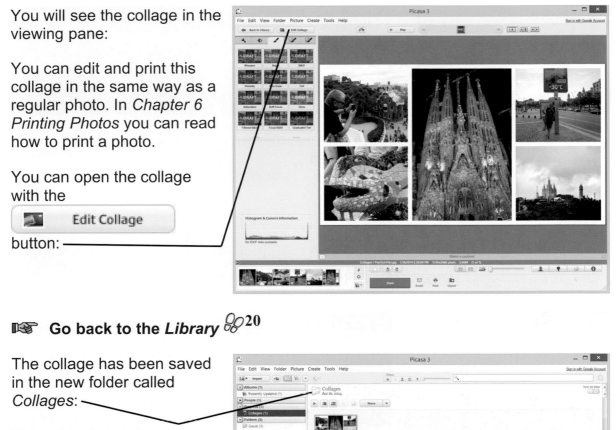

You can open the collage with the

button: ──────

☞ **Go back to the *Library*** 🦶²⁰

The collage has been saved in the new folder called *Collages*: ─────

This folder is located on your computer in the *Picasa* folder within the *(My) Pictures* folder.

☞ **Empty the Photo Tray** 🦶⁴⁶

4.2 Viewing Photos in a Slideshow

Instead of viewing the photos in a folder in the *Library* one by one, you can also view them in a slideshow.

☞ **Open the**  **Practice-Files folder** 🦶⁹

☞ **Click the first photo**

☞ **Click**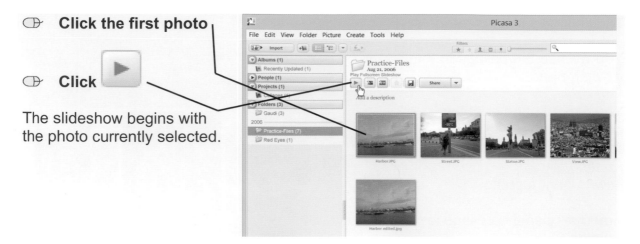

The slideshow begins with the photo currently selected.

You will see the first photo full screen, and after a few seconds you will see the next photo:

☞ **Move the mouse pointer**

At the bottom you will see a toolbar, and the video has stoped playing:

The toolbar contains a number of buttons. This is what they do:

 Start or continue playing. You should not move the mouse pointer while the slideshow plays.

 Skip to the previous or the next slide.

Rotate a photo to the left or to the right.

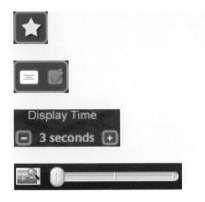

Star the photo.

Display or hide the titles of photos.

Set the display time per slide.

Slider for zooming in or out.

Start the slideshow once again:

☞ **Click**

The photos in the folder will appear one by one. The last photo will remain frozen on your screen. This is how you go back to *Picasa*:

☞ **Click**

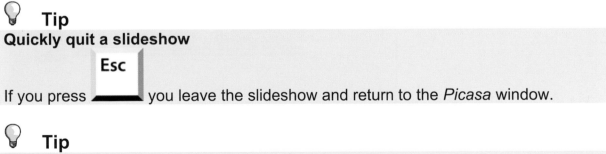

You will see the *Picasa* window again.

♀ **Tip**
Quickly quit a slideshow

Esc

If you press ▂▂▂▂ you leave the slideshow and return to the *Picasa* window.

♀ **Tip**
Music
You can also play background music while watching a slideshow. In the *Tips* at the end of this chapter you can read how to add music.

4.3 Create a Gift CD

If you want to show your friends and family a large collection of photos you can create a gift CD or DVD with a slideshow:

☞ **Open the** 📁 **Practice-Files** folder 👣⁹

🖐 **Please note:**

You can only include entire albums or folders in a slideshow, you cannot use individual photos. That is why you need to collect the photos you want to use in the slideshow first, and place them together in a folder or album. The best thing to do is create a whole new album for this purpose. You can delete this album afterwards if you want. You can go back to *Chapter 1 Setting up Picasa* to learn how to do this.

☞ **Click Create**

☞ **Click**
Create a Gift CD

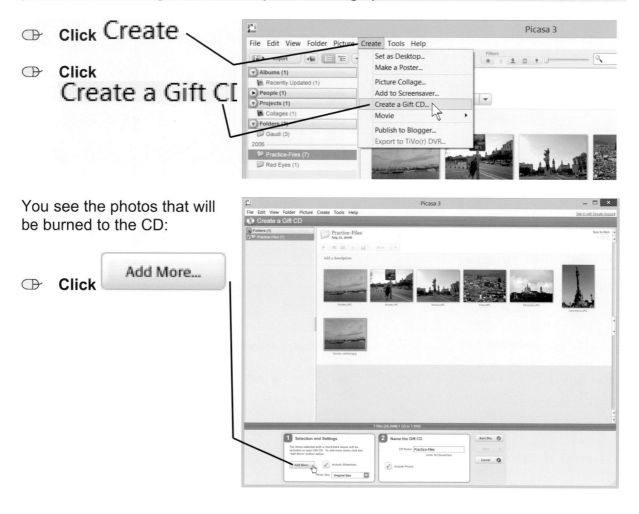

You see the photos that will be burned to the CD:

☞ **Click** Add More...

☞ **Check the box** ☑ **by the** 🗀 Gaudi (3) **folder**

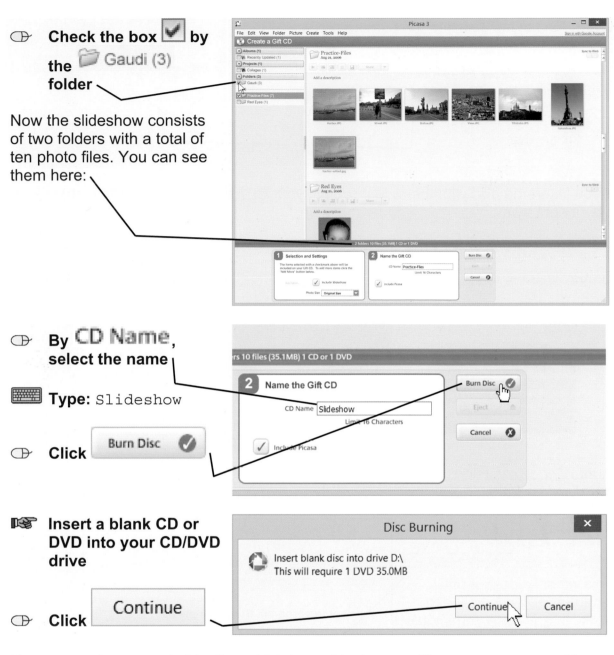

Now the slideshow consists of two folders with a total of ten photo files. You can see them here:

☞ **By** CD Name, **select the name**

⌨ **Type:** Slideshow

☞ **Click** Burn Disc ✓

☞ **Insert a blank CD or DVD into your CD/DVD drive**

☞ **Click** Continue

If you are using a rewritable disc which is not blank, you will see a message asking you whether the disc can be erased. In that case you click Erase Disc .

On the right-hand side of your window you will see a progress bar:

When *Picasa* has finished the burning process:

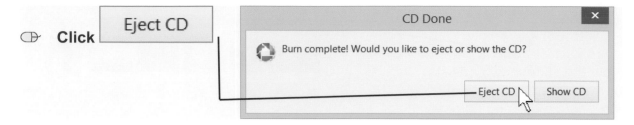

⊕ **Click** [Eject CD]

If you insert the disc with the slideshow into your CD/DVD drive you will be able to play it right away:

☞ **Insert the disc into the CD/DVD drive**

On the desktop in *Windows 8.1*:

In the top right-hand corner of the window:

⊕ **Click**

> **DVD RW Drive (D:) Slideshow**
> Tap to choose what happens with this disc

In all *Windows* versions you will now see a window with the options you can use for this disc:

⊕ **Click**
Run PicasaCD.exe

This window looks a bit different in *Windows 7* and *Vista*. In any case you should click the
Run PicasaCD.exe
option.

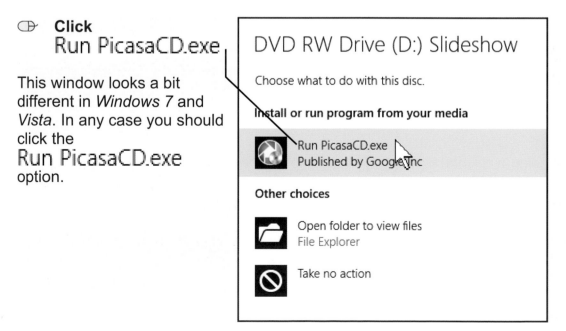

By clicking an image you can display the photos in that folder:

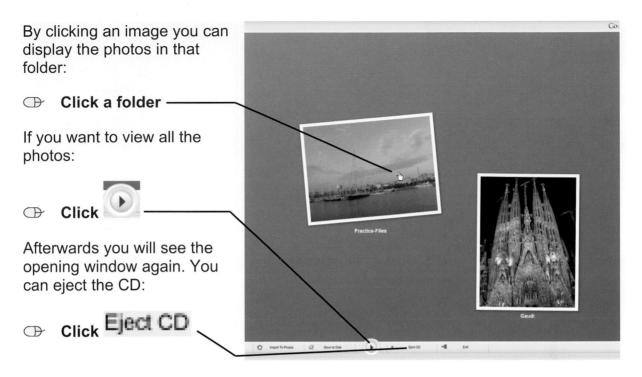

☞ **Click a folder**

If you want to view all the photos:

☞ **Click** ▶

Afterwards you will see the opening window again. You can eject the CD:

☞ **Click** Eject CD

The CD is ejected and the slideshow will stop.

➥ Please note:
The gift CD can be played on many different DVD players. But some older players may not recognize the disc and therefore, will not be able to play it.

4.4 Turning a Slideshow into a Video

The gift CD you previously created can be played in a DVD player. However, you can also turn a slideshow into a video that can be played with *Windows Media Player* and certain other programs.

➥ Please note:
A video that you have made with a video camera, or downloaded from the Internet, is called a video clip in *Picasa*. In *Picasa*, a video is a combination of photos, video clips, and sound, which is saved and played as a single entity.

First you need to create a new album with the photos you want to use in the video. In order to do this, you need to place a few photos in the Photo Tray:

☞ **Open the**  **Gaudi (3) folder** ⸜⸝[9]

☞ **Place** ___ **and** ___ **in the Photo Tray** $\mathcal{QQ}^{22}$

☞ **Open the** 🗁 Practice-Files **folder** $\mathcal{QQ}^{9}$

☞ **Place** ___ **and** ___ **in the Photo Tray** $\mathcal{QQ}^{22}$

Now you can create a new album with these photos:

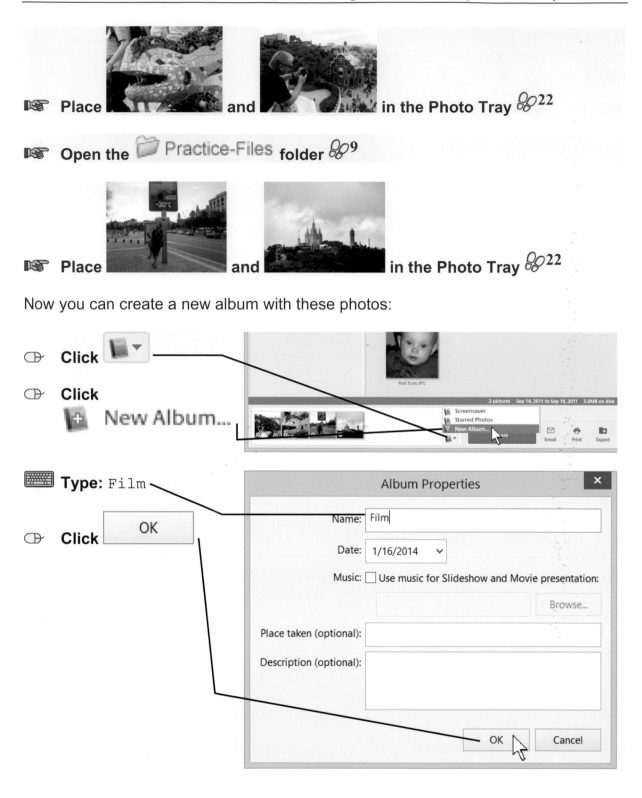

⊕ **Click** ___

⊕ **Click**
　➕ New Album...

⌨ **Type:** Film

⊕ **Click** OK

The  Film (4) album has been added:

You no longer need the photos in the Photo Tray:

👉 **Empty the Photo Tray** 🐾**46**

This is how you create a video:

👉 **Open the** Film (4) **album** 🐾**9**

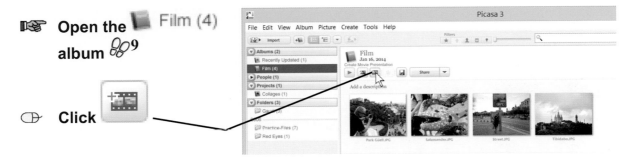

👉 **Click** ⊞📽

Picasa will automatically turn the photos in the album into a video, and add a title slide at the start. Take a look at the video first:

👉 **Click** ▶

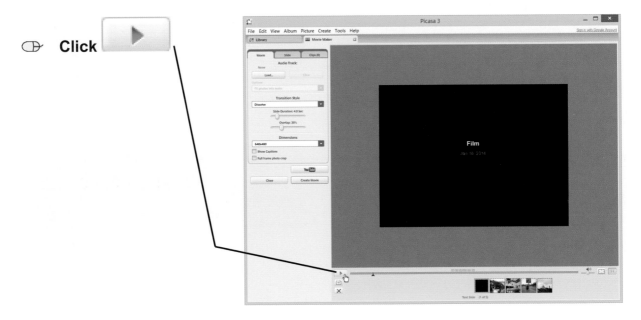

The video is played. You can pause the video by clicking the ⏸ button. When you want to continue, click the ▶ button.

At this stage you can still edit the video. This is how you remove photos from the video without removing them from the album itself:

☞ **Click**

You will see the photo:

☞ **Click** ✕

The photo has been removed.

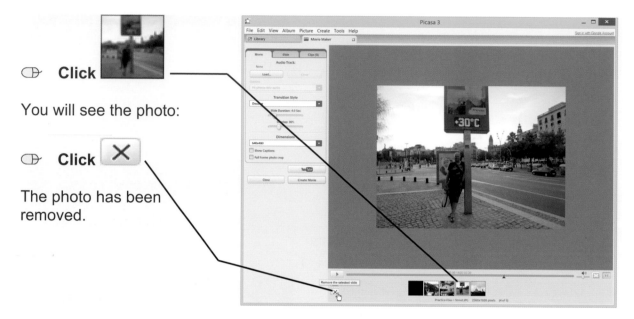

You can also add new photos. This is done on the *Clips* tab:

☞ **Click the**
   Clips (1)   **tab**

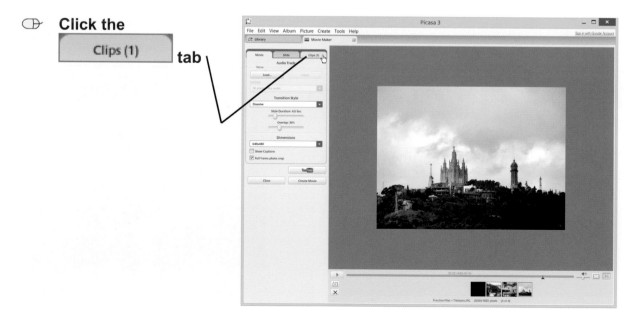

You will see the photo you have removed: ─────

You can select another photo from a different folder:

⊕ **Click**

Get More...

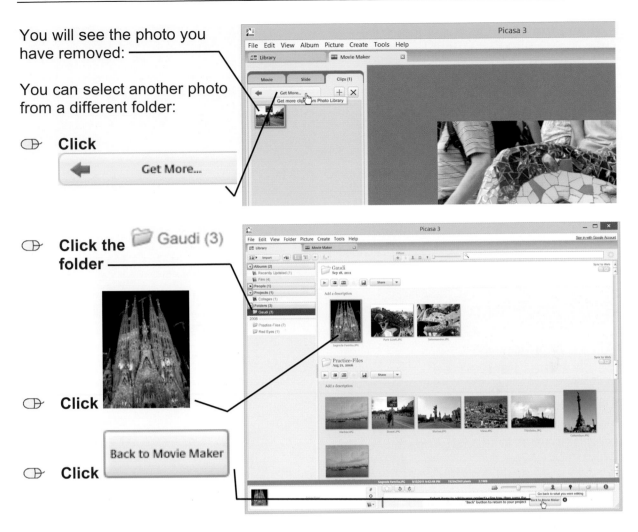

⊕ **Click the** 📁 Gaudi (3) **folder** ─────

⊕ **Click**

⊕ **Click** Back to Movie Maker

💡 **Tip**

Add multiple photos
If you want to add multiple photos at once, you need to place these in the Photo Tray too.

You will see the photo you added in the overview: ─────

Now add the photo to the video:

👉 **Drag the photo to a spot immediately after the title slide**

The photo has been added:

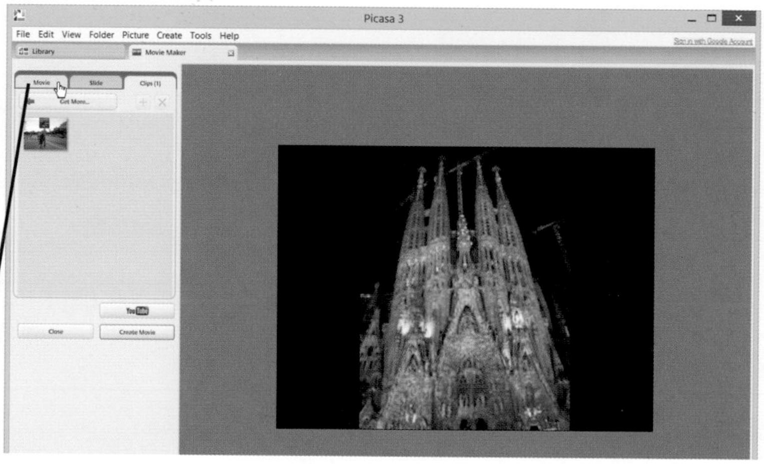

Due to the fact that this photo was taken vertically you will see a black bar to the left and right of the photo.

👉 **Click the**

  Movie **tab**

👉 **Check the box ☑ by Full frame photo cro**

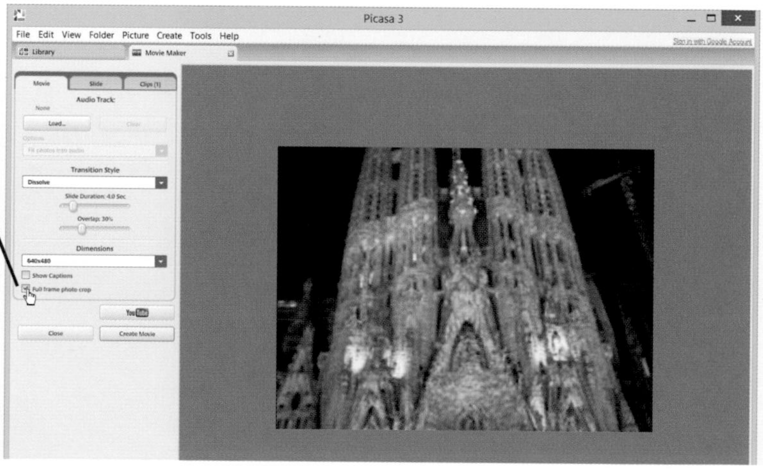

Now the photo will fill the entire frame. Because you have cropped the photo, parts of the top and bottom have been cut off.

Unfortunately, this window does not allow you to select the part of the photo you want to keep. And you cannot undo this operation. You can only remove the photo from the video, and add it again on the *Clips* tab. If you want to display a specific part of a photo full screen, it is better to do the editing first (using the cropping option for example) before adding the photo to a video.

⍾ Tip

Does the photo seem unclear?
Sometimes the photo you have added will look a bit blurry in this window. You can solve this problem by briefly clicking another photo, and then clicking the previous photo again. This will render the photo sharp again.

4.5 Editing and Adding Title Slides

When you create a video in *Picasa*, the program will automatically add a title slide at the beginning of the video. This is how you edit the slide on the *Slide* tab:

☞ **Click the**   Slide   **tab**

☞ **Click the title slide**

☞ **Select the text**

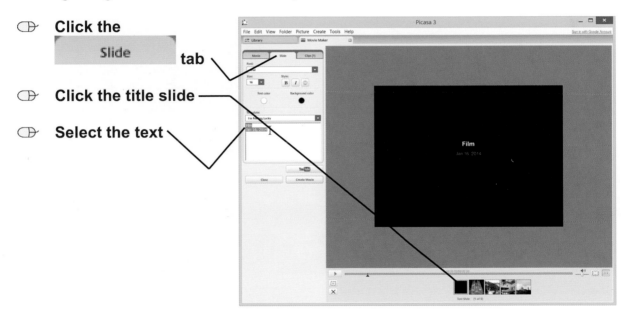

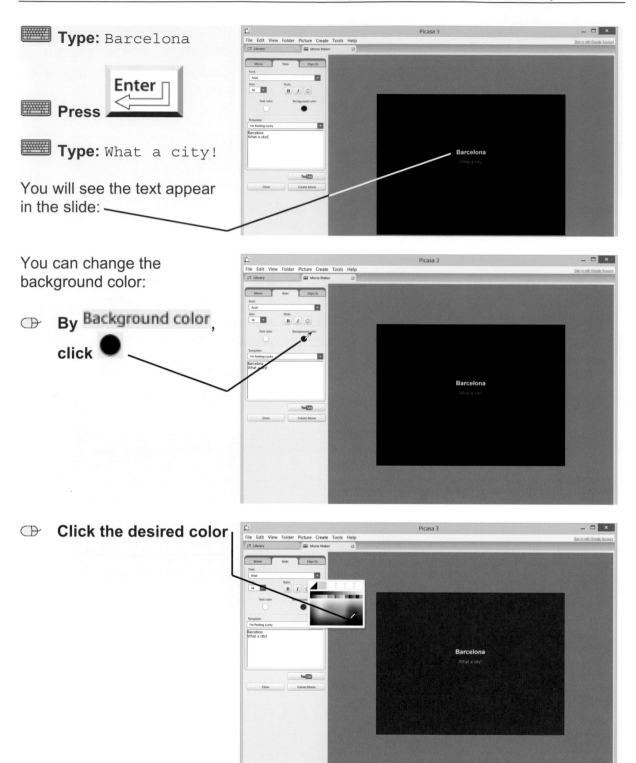

Type: Barcelona

Press Enter

Type: What a city!

You will see the text appear in the slide:

You can change the background color:

👆 **By** Background color, **click** ●

👆 **Click the desired color**

You can change the color of the text too:

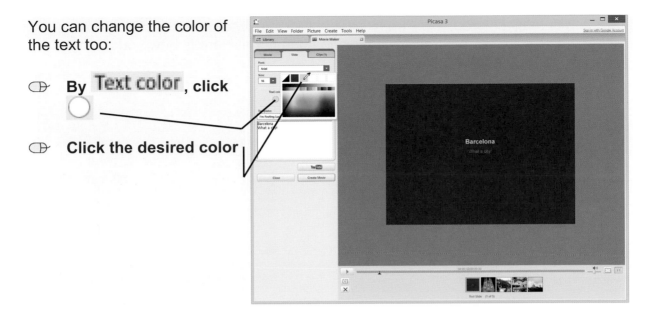

⬭ **By** Text color **, click**

⬭ **Click the desired color**

Instead of using a separate title slide you can also add text to an existing photo and use this photo as a title slide. First, you need to remove the current title slide:

In the bottom left-hand corner of the window:

⬭ **Click** ✕

You will see the next photo:

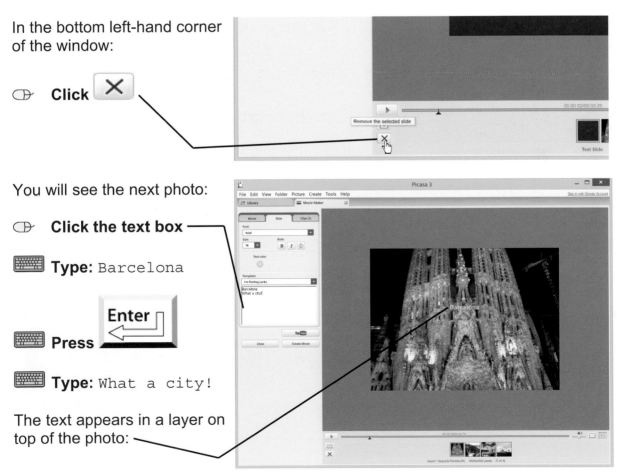

⬭ **Click the text box**

⌨ **Type:** Barcelona

⌨ **Press** Enter

⌨ **Type:** What a city!

The text appears in a layer on top of the photo:

If a photo is multi-colored, it will be difficult to find a text color that is clearly visible. In this case it may be better to place the text in a template. Here is how you do that:

☞ By Template:, click ▼

☞ Click
   Gradient - Black

Now you will see the title
more clearly:

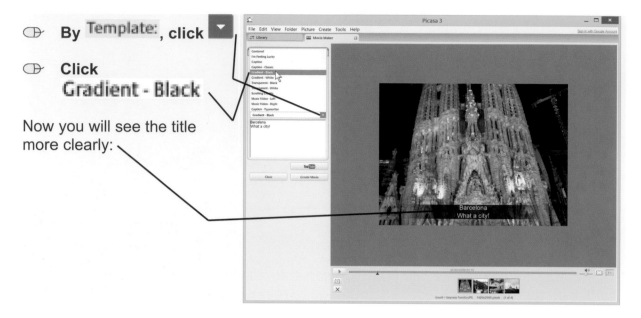

You can also adjust the text formatting, just like you do in other programs:

- By Font: you use ▼ to select a different font.

- By Size: you use ▼ to select a different font size.

- With B you can make the title bold, or disable the bold lettering.

- With I you can italicize the title, or disable the italics.

- With ◎ you will only see the outline of the letters, or you will see the original letters again.

- You can change the text color again with ◯, by Text color.

💡 Tip

Insert a title slide

If you decide to add a separate title slide later on, or if you want to enter a (sub)title slide between certain slides, you can insert your own title slide:

☞ **Click** 🖼️

You will see a title slide:

☞ **Type the text for the slide and**

☞ **Select the color for the text** 🐾67

☞ **Drag the slide to the correct position**

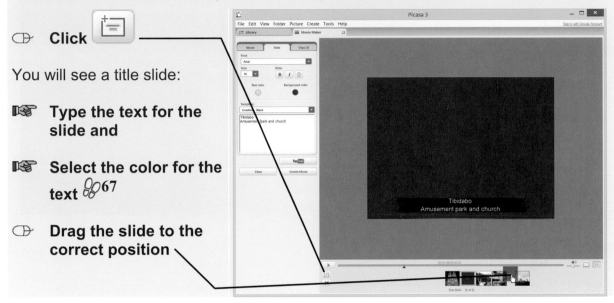

4.6 Setting the View and Transitions for the Video

If you have created a video of your slideshow, you can also set the style for the transitions between the slides. The transition you choose will be used for all the slides:

☞ **Click the** **Movie** **tab**

☞ **Play the video** 🐾47

Pay close attention to the transitions between the slides.

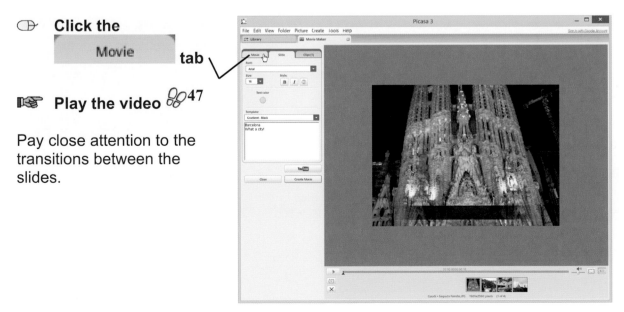

By default, the transition style called *Dissolve* has been selected. You can easily set another transition style between the slides. For example:

☞ **By** Transition Style, click ▼

☞ **Click** Pan and Zoom

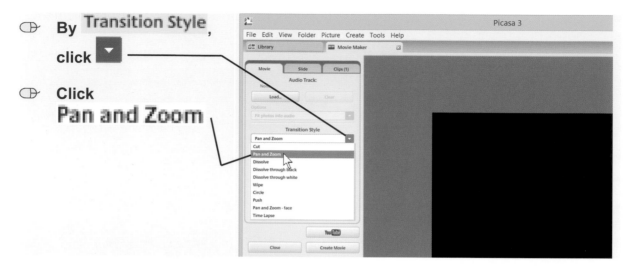

☞ **Play the video once again** 🦶47

You will see that this type of transition makes the slideshow look livelier. Try out another style:

☞ **By** Transition Style, click ▼

☞ **Click** Circle

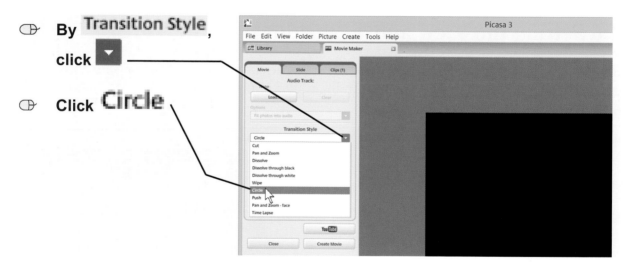

☞ **Play the video once again** 🦶47

Now the new slide will appear within a circle which will be projected in front of the previous slide.

Set the slide duration:

☞ **Drag the slider** 🖱 **by**
Slide Duration: 4.0 S
to the right until you
see
Slide Duration: 6.0 S

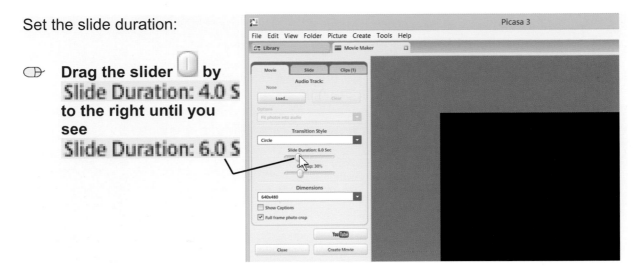

☞ **Play the video once again** 🐾**47**

Now a slide will be displayed for a little while longer, before switching to the next slide.

You can also adjust the amount of time the transitions take:

☞ **Drag the slider** 🖱 **by**
Overlap: 30% **to the**
right until you see
Overlap: 80%

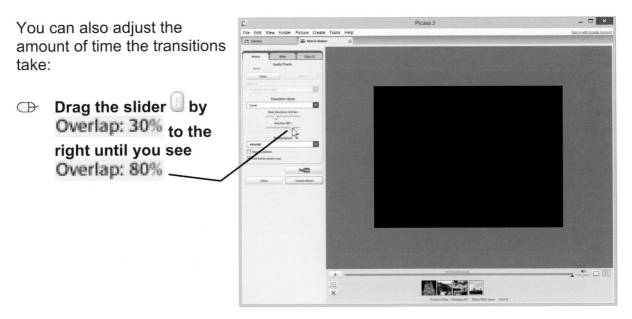

☞ **Play the video once again** 🐾**47**

The transition period is now a bit longer and you can see the transition more clearly.

🔆 Tip
Dimensions

By **Dimensions** you select the screen resolution for which the video will be created. If you select a high resolution the images will be much sharper but the file will become larger. And the video may not be so easily displayed on older computers with a lower screen resolution. This is how you select the dimensions:

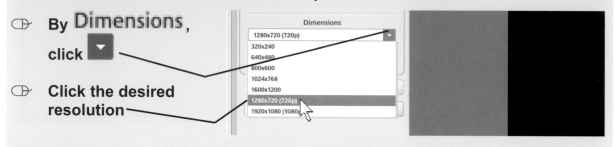

- ☞ **By Dimensions**, **click** ▼

- ☞ **Click the desired resolution**

The 1280 x 720 resolution is a popular and frequently used resolution for screens of standard quality. 1920 x 1080 is used for larger HD screens.

4.7 Adding Music to Videos

The music you add to a video will be saved together with the video, and will always be audible whenever you play the video. You can use either MP3 or WMA music files. In this example we have used the audio file that is included in the *Practice-Files* folder. If you followed the steps to save the practice files as described in *Chapter 1 Setting up Picasa* you will find this file in the (*My*) *Music* folder.

You are going to add music to your slideshow:

- ☞ **Click**

    Load...

Open the (*My*) *Music* folder:

⊕ **Click** 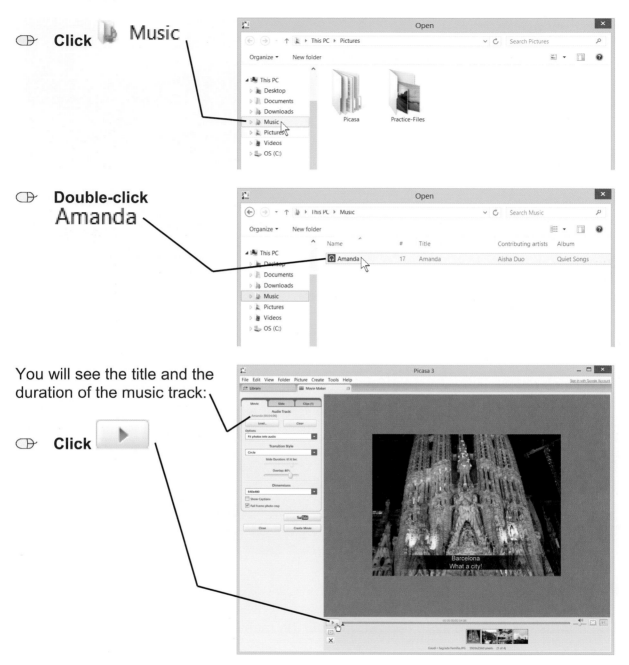 Music

⊕ **Double-click**
Amanda

You will see the title and the
duration of the music track:

⊕ **Click**

The slideshow will be played, but the length of the slideshow will be adapted to the duration of the music track. That is why it takes a long time before the second slide is displayed.

When the second slide appears:

⊕ **Click**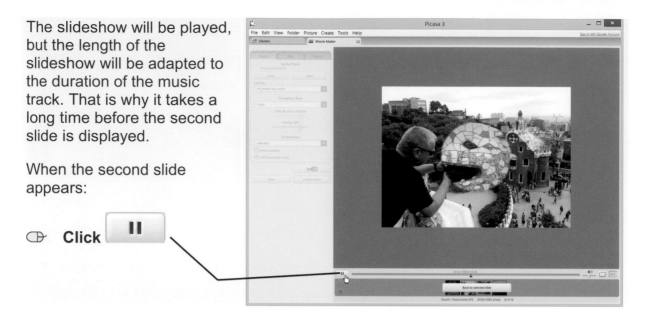

You can allow the slides to repeat until the music has finished:

⊕ **By** Options**, click**

⊕ **Click**
Loop photos to match audio

☞ **Play the video** **47**

The photos will be displayed repeatedly until the music has finished.

☞ **Stop playing the video** 🐾**48**

A third option is to stop the music track as soon as the slideshow has finished:

☞ By Options , click ▼

☞ Click
Truncate audio

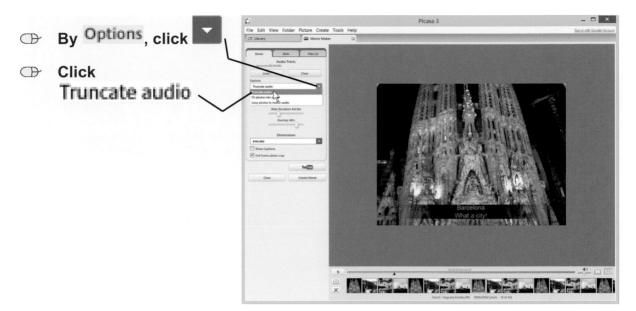

☞ **Play the video** ♋47

Now the music will stop playing when the slideshow has finished. The *truncate audio* option is especially suitable if you use neutral background music.

4.8 Saving and Playing Videos

After you have finished creating the video you can save it, like this:

☞ **Click**

Create Movie

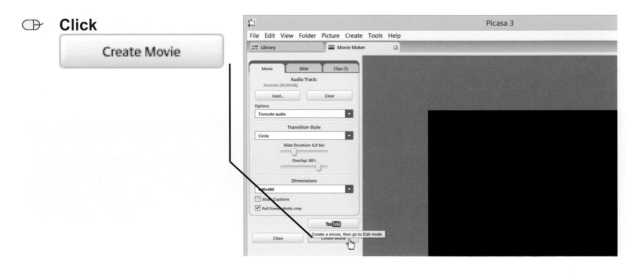

During the creation of the video you will see a progress bar in the bottom right-hand corner of the screen:

Please note: if the video is very long, this may take a while.

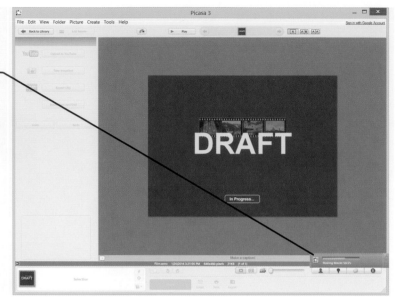

Afterwards, the video will be played automatically:

☞ **Go back to the *Library*** 🐾²⁰

The video has been included in a project ⊞ Movies (1):

Play the video once again:

☞ **Click** ⊞ Movies (1)

☞ **Click** ▶

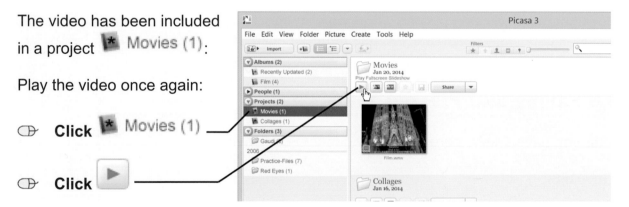

Now the video will be played full-screen. After the video has finished, the screen will turn dark:

☞ **Move the mouse pointer**

☞ **Click** ← Exit

The video is finished but you can still edit it. In the next section you will learn how to crop a video clip. Then you will add this clip to the video.

4.9 Cropping Video Clips

You cannot edit video clips in *Picasa* but you can crop them. First, add the video clip to *Picasa*:

⊕ **Click** File

⊕ **Click** Add File to Picasa

You can save the video clip in the (*My*) *Videos* folder:

⊕ **Click** Videos

⊕ **Double-click** Video

⊕ **Click** Olympic Stadium Barcelona

⊕ **Click** Open

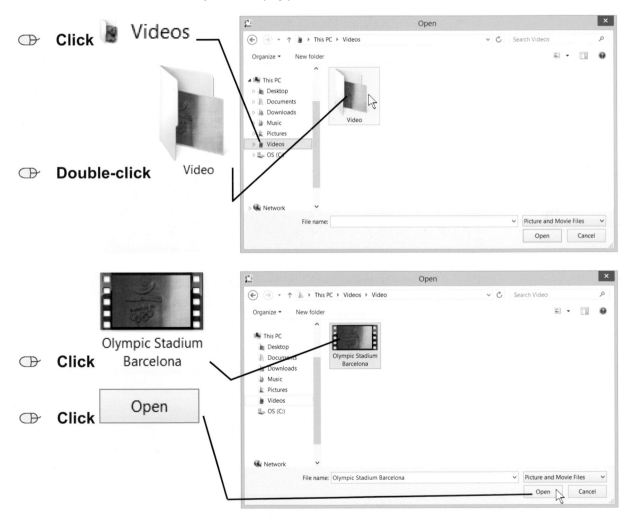

⏘ **Click** Video (1)

Play the video clip:

⏘ **Double-click**

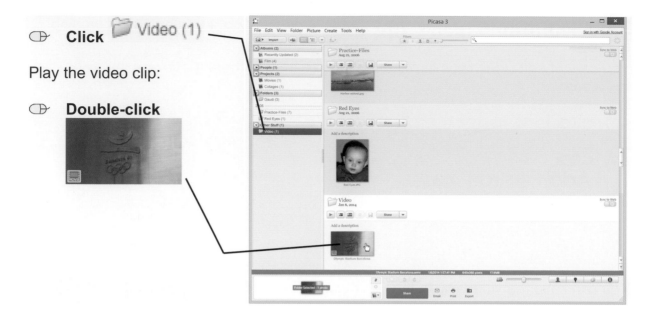

You will see the video clip:

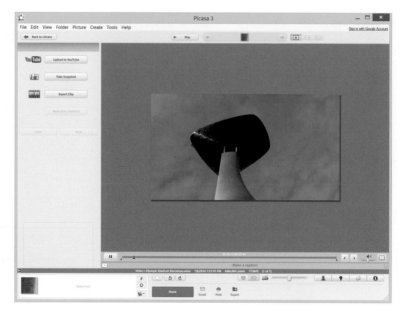

If your video clip is too long you can shorten it by creating new starting and ending points:

☞ **Play the video once again** ⅋47

To create a starting point:

☞ **Click** [▲] **while the video plays**

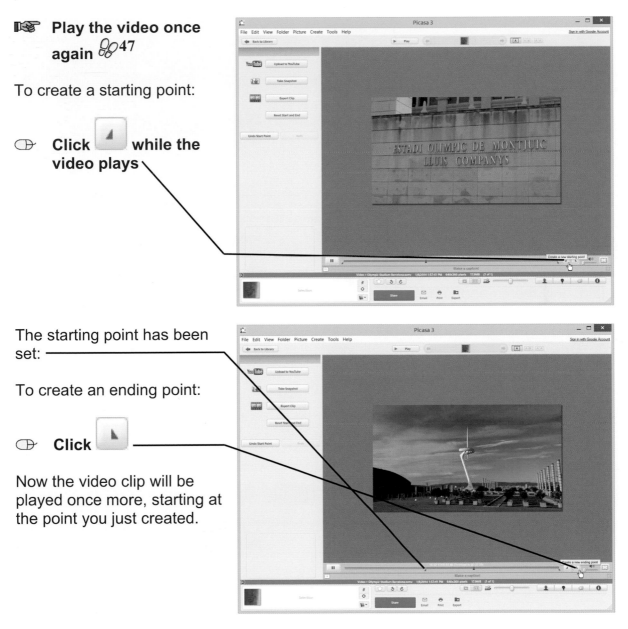

The starting point has been set:

To create an ending point:

☞ **Click** [▲]

Now the video clip will be played once more, starting at the point you just created.

💡 Tip

Pause and drag

If you are not satisfied with the starting and ending points you have just created, you can adjust them by dragging them on the time bar below the clip. You can also do this when the video is paused. You can continue to pause and drag to make adjustments until you have the starting and ending points you want.

The ending point has been set: ──────

☞ **Click**

[⬅ Back to Library]

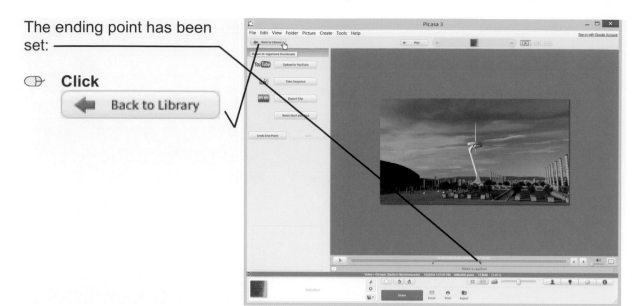

When you play the video clip again, only the cropped part will be played:

☞ **Double-click**

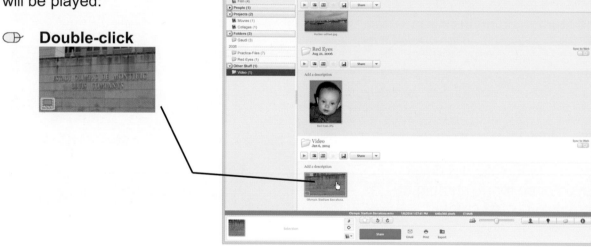

You will only see the part you have cropped:

Now you can save this clip as a separate video clip:

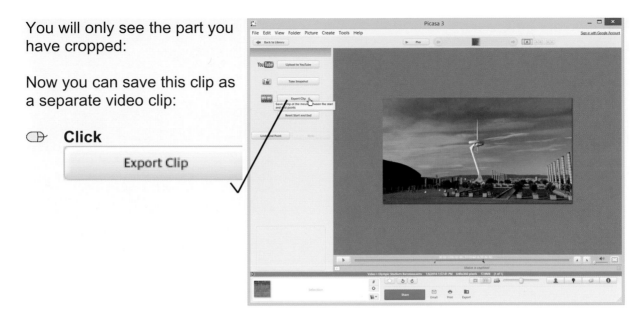

⊕ **Click**

Export Clip

The cropped clip will be saved as a new video clip:

During the saving process, a progress bar is displayed:

Once the new video clip is saved, you can delete the starting and ending points in the original video, in order to play the video in its full length. You can do that as follows:

⊕ **Click**

Reset Start and End

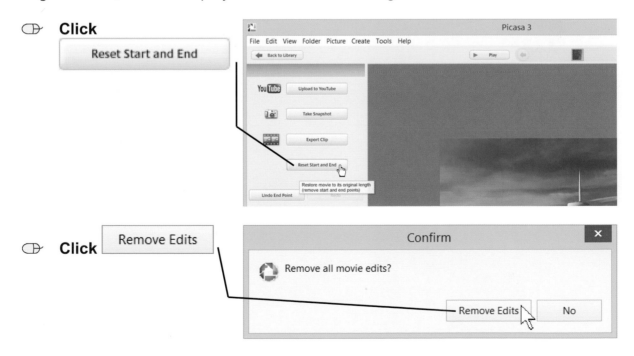

⊕ **Click** Remove Edits

The markers have been deleted:

👉 **Click**

    ⬅ **Back to Library**

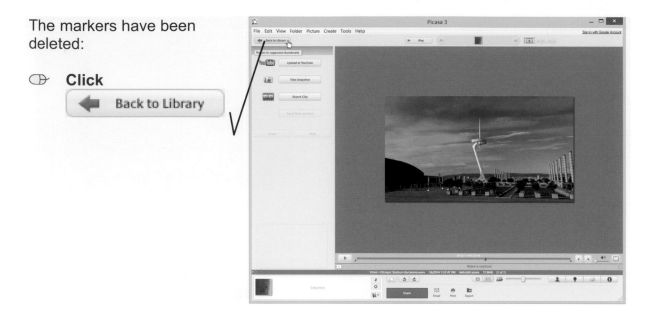

The exported video has been saved in a folder that is not scanned by *Picasa,* that is to say, not with the current settings. In *Chapter 1 Setting up Picasa* you had only added the folder with sample photos to the scan list. Here is how you add the folder containing the exported video:

👉 **Click** File

👉 **Click**
    Add Folder to Pica

⊕ **If necessary, drag the scroll bar upwards**

⊕ **By** 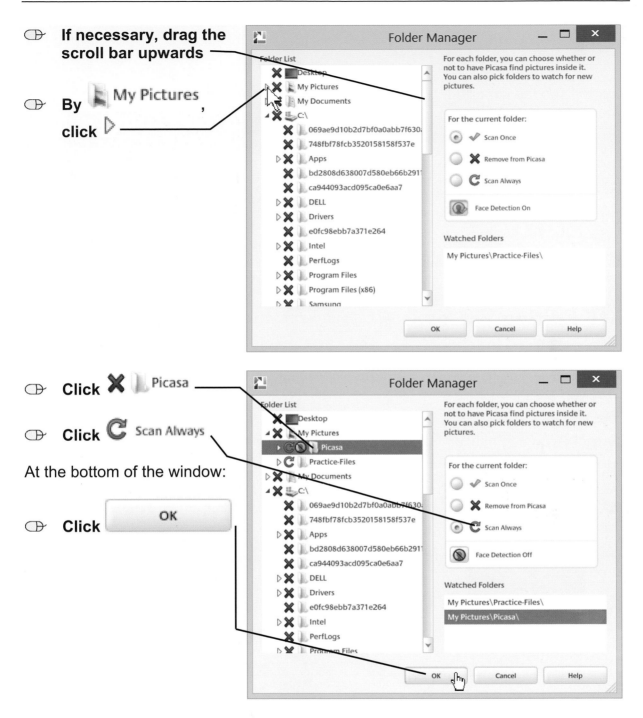 **My Pictures,**

click ▷

⊕ **Click ✖ 📁 Picasa**

⊕ **Click ⟳ Scan Always**

At the bottom of the window:

⊕ **Click** OK

👈 **Click**

⬛ Exported Videos (1)

You will see the exported video:

4.10 Editing Videos

You can still edit a video, even after you have finished it. You can add or remove other photos, title slides and other video clips as well.

➥ **Please note:**

Currently you can only edit the videos you have created in *Picasa*. It is not possible to edit other types of video clips.

👉 **Open the** ⬛ Movies (1) **project** 🐾⁹

👈 **Double-click**

Film.wmv

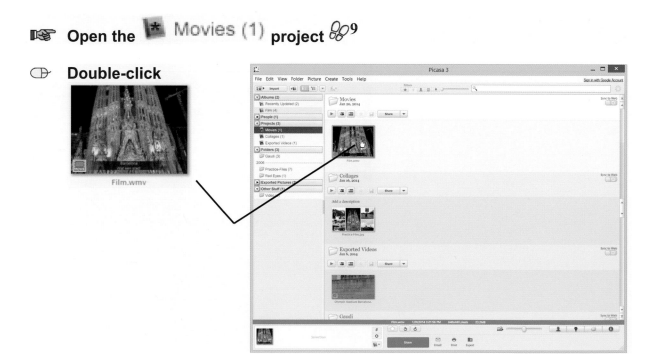

The video is played.
If the video is taking too long

you can press the button.

After the video has been played:

⊕ **Click**

Edit Movie

⊕ **Click the**

Clips (0)

tab

⊕ **Click**

Get More...

☞ **Open the**

★ Exported Videos (1)

project ✇⁹

⊕ **Click**

Olympic Stadium Barcelona.

Back to Movie Maker

⊕ **Click**

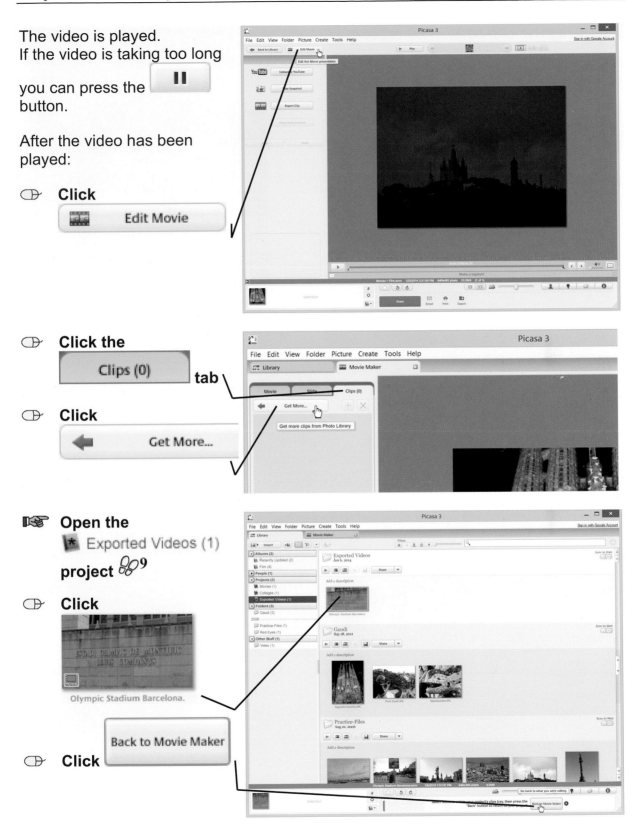

- **Drag the clip to a position between the second and third photo**

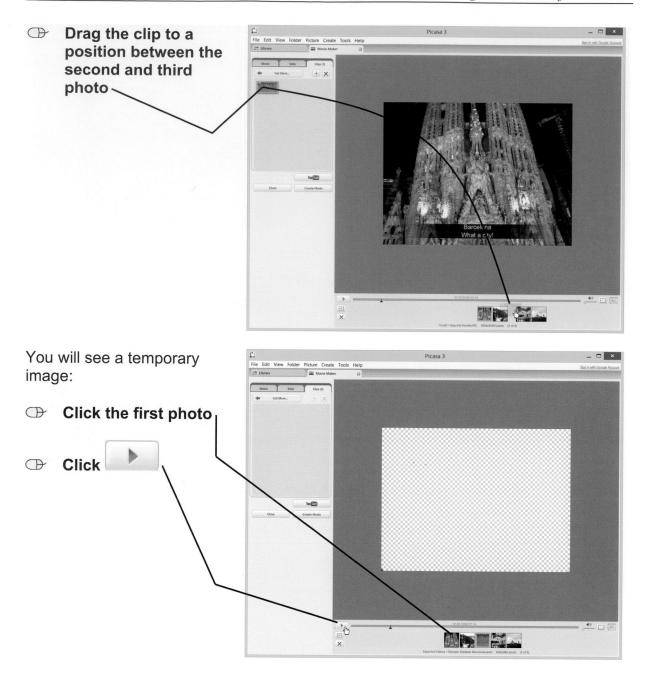

You will see a temporary image:

- **Click the first photo**

- **Click** [▶]

The video will be played, including the video clip.

You can create a new video from this material:

Click **Create Movie**

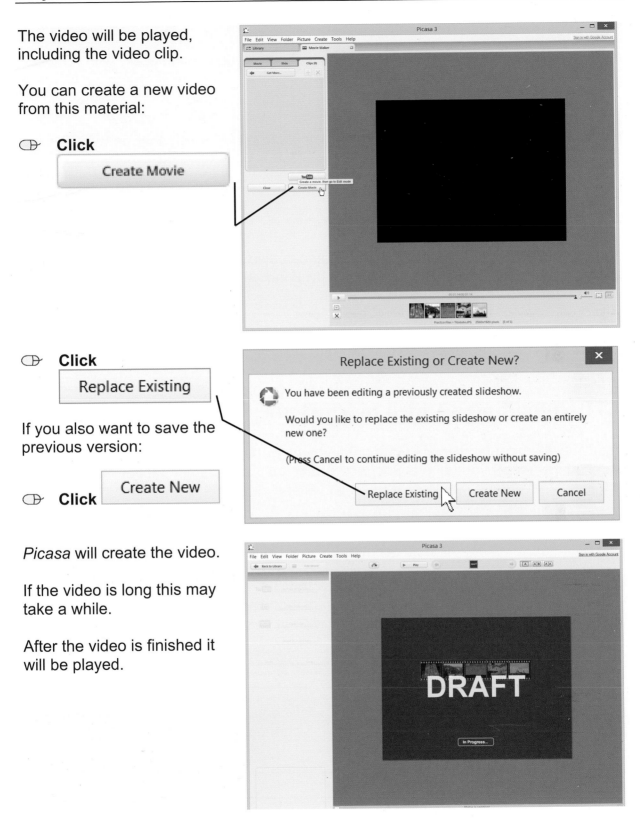

Click **Replace Existing**

If you also want to save the previous version:

Click **Create New**

Picasa will create the video.

If the video is long this may take a while.

After the video is finished it will be played.

Please note:

If you add the video to a gift CD/DVD, it cannot be played automatically with *Picasa*.

In this case you can only play the video by opening the Movies folder on the CD or

DVD in *File Explorer*. You will find this subfolder in the Pictures folder.

The video will be saved as a .WMV file. You can also view this file with other programs such as *Windows Media Player*. In *Windows 8.1* you can also view the video in the *Photos* and *Video* apps.

If you have installed specific burning software to your computer such as *DVD Maker* or *Nero*, you can burn the video to a CD or a DVD.

4.11 Uploading a Video to YouTube

YouTube is a popular website that contains a huge number of videos that can be watched for free. If you have a *Google* account you can also upload your own videos. In this way, everyone can view your project online.

Please note:

You will need to have a *Google* account if you want to upload videos to *YouTube*. If you do not have such an account, then click the [⬅ Back to Library] button and just read through the next section. If you want, you can create a *Google* account on the www.google.com website. Then click the *Sign in* button to sign in.

Click

[Upload to YouTube]

Sign in with your *Google* or *YouTube* account:

⌨ **By Email, type your email address**

⌨ **By Password, type your password**

🖰 **Click**

If your *Google* account has not yet been linked to a *YouTube* account, you will see this window:

🖰 **Click** Yes

If your *Google* account is linked to a *YouTube* account, continue further on page 192.

⌨ **Type your password**

🖰 **Click**

Google will need some additional information from you. This information is used to create a *YouTube* channel and a *Google+* profile for you. *Google+* is *Google's* social network. On page 230 of this book you can find extra information about the free storage space you get with your *Google+* account.

💡 Tip

Delete a Google+ profile
If you do not want to use *Google+* you can delete the profile again. In the *Tips* at the end of this chapter you can read how to do this.

☞ **Click**
Skip for now

☞ **Fill in your password again and sign in**

In this example the *YouTube* account is associated with a different name:

☞ **Click** click here.

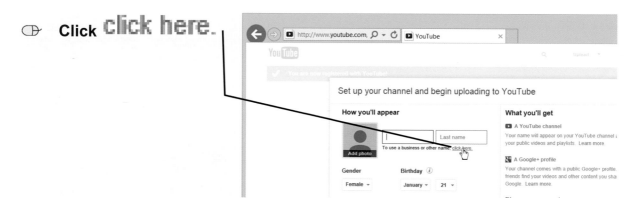

☞ **Fill in the name of your channel**

☞ **Select the category**

☞ **Select who your content is appropriate for**

☞ **Check the box ☑ by I agree to the Pages**

☞ **Click** Done

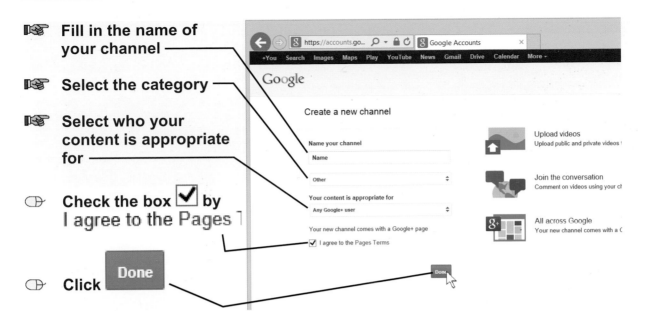

You will see your *YouTube* channel:

☞ **Click** ✕

You will now see the email address you signed in with in the top right-hand corner of your *Picasa* window. You can sign out now:

☞ **Click** Sign Out

Your movie has not yet been uploaded. Try again:

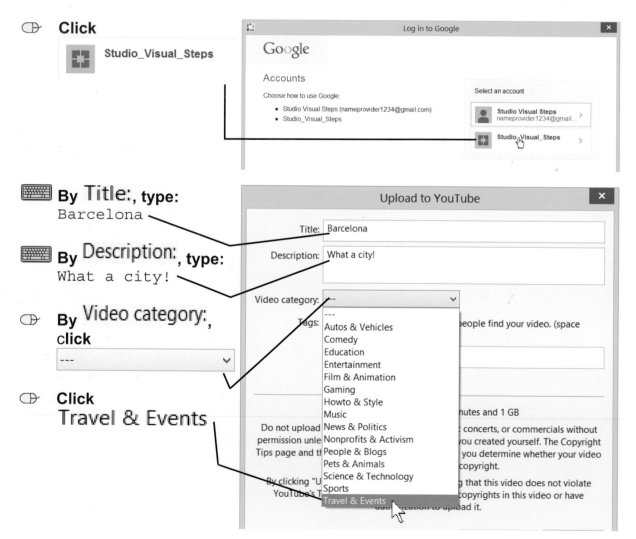

⊕ **Click**

Upload to YouTube

☞ **Sign in again** ⮑⁵⁶

Since your *YouTube* account has a different name than your *Google* account, select the other name here:

⊕ **Click**

⊞ Studio_Visual_Steps

⌨ By **Title:**, type: Barcelona

⌨ By **Description:**, type: What a city!

⊕ By **Video category:**, click

⊕ **Click** Travel & Events

⌨ **By** Tags: **, type:**
Barcelona Spain
Gaudi

☞ **Click**

Upload Video

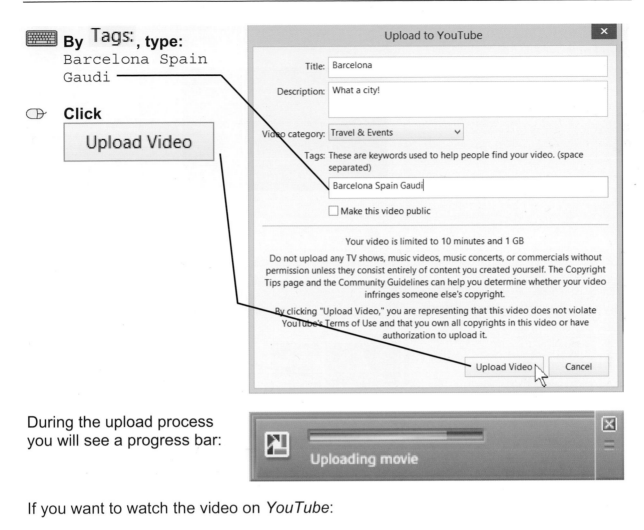

During the upload process
you will see a progress bar:

If you want to watch the video on *YouTube*:

☞ **Click** Film.wmv

You will see your video appear on your *YouTube* channel:

☞ **If necessary, sign in
with your account**
👣56

☞ **Click**

Your video is played on *YouTube*:

After the video has finished playing you can sign out from *YouTube*:

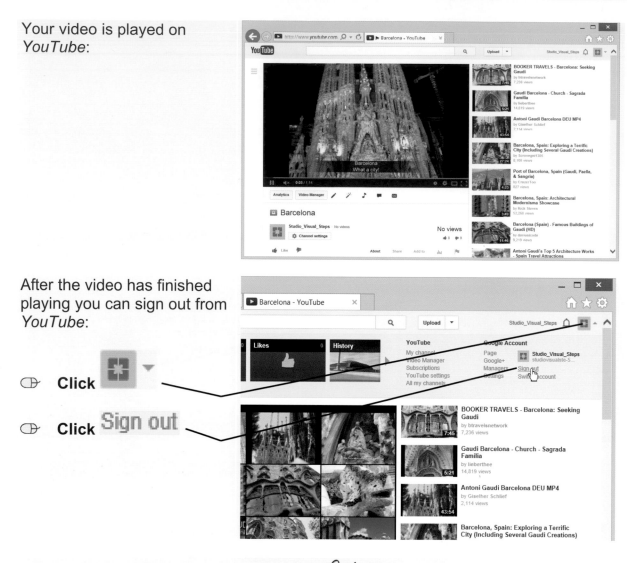

☞ **Click**

☞ **Click** Sign out

☞ **Close the *Internet Explorer* window** ᴼᴼ4

☞ **Go back to the *Library*** ᴼᴼ20

Now you will see that the *Picasa* window has changed a bit:

In the top right-hand corner you will see a different email address:

At the bottom, this button has appeared

This will happen if your *YouTube* account is also associated with a *Google+* account.

You can sign out:

☞ **Click** Sign Out

You have signed out from *Google* account:

4.12 Using Photos as a Screensaver

Picasa uses a special album for the photos that can be used as a screensaver. To create a screensaver, you first select the folder or album that will be used:

☞ **Open the** 📁 Gaudi (3) **album** 👣**9**

☞ **Click Create**

☞ **Click Add to Screensaver**

☞ **Click** Yes

You may still see some wrong images in this example:

☞ **Click** Settings...

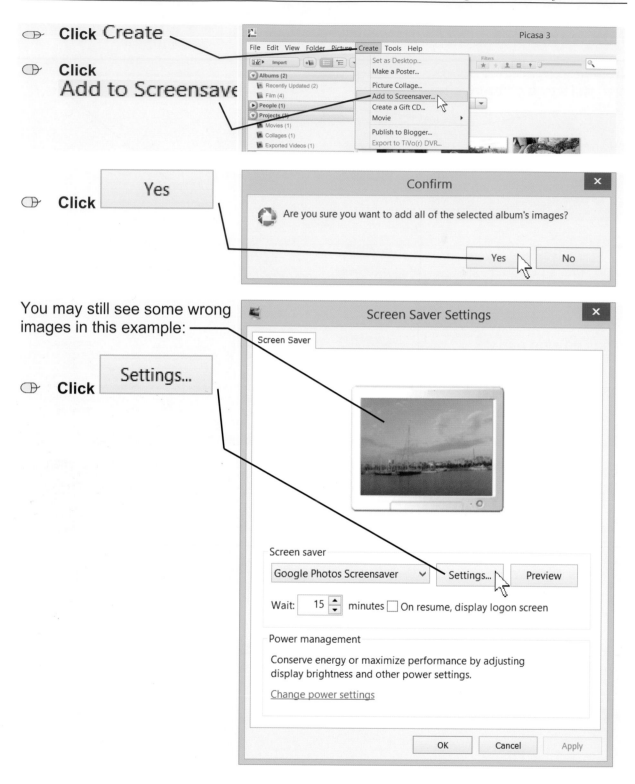

If you only want to use the photos in the 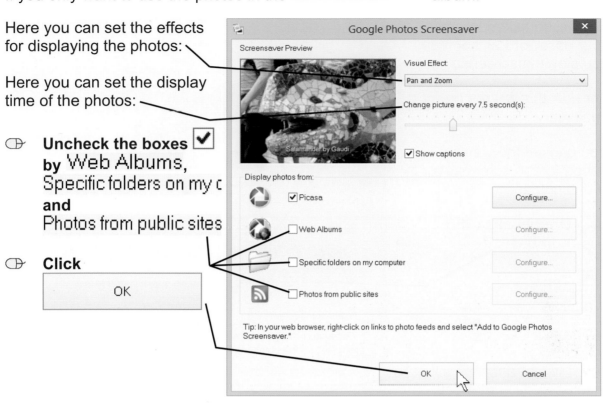 Screensaver (3) album:

Here you can set the effects
for displaying the photos:

Here you can set the display
time of the photos:

⊕ **Uncheck the boxes** ✔
   by Web Albums,
   Specific folders on my c
   and
   Photos from public sites

⊕ **Click**

   OK

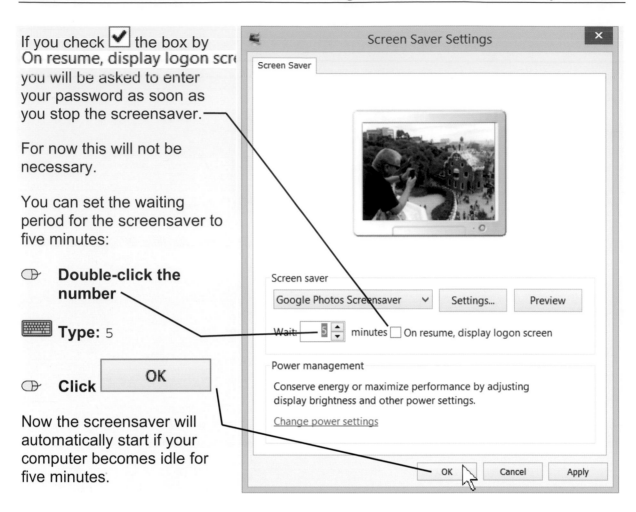

If you check ☑ the box by
On resume, display logon scre
you will be asked to enter
your password as soon as
you stop the screensaver.

For now this will not be
necessary.

You can set the waiting
period for the screensaver to
five minutes:

☞ **Double-click the
   number**

⌨ **Type:** 5

☞ **Click** OK

Now the screensaver will
automatically start if your
computer becomes idle for
five minutes.

4.13 Setting a Photo as a Desktop Background

It is very easy to use *Picasa* to set up a photo or a collage as your desktop
background (also called wallpaper). Just give it a try:

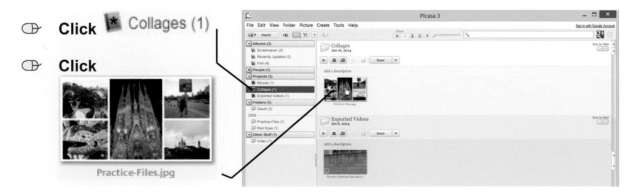

☞ **Click** ⬛ Collages (1)

☞ **Click**

Practice-Files.jpg

☞ **Click** Create

☞ **Click** Set as Desktop...

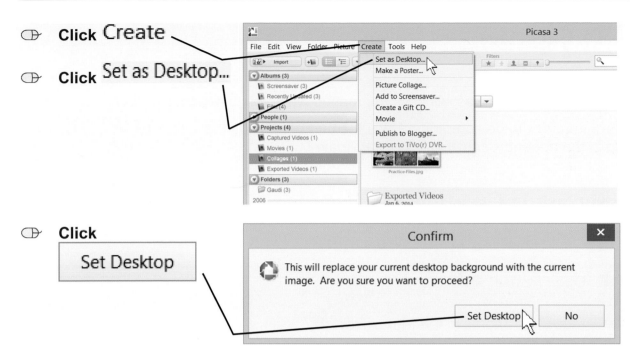

☞ **Click**

Set Desktop

Now the collage has been set as your desktop background.

4.14 Exercises

The following exercises will help you master what you just learned. Have you forgotten how to do something? Use the number beside the footsteps ❧[1] to look it up in the appendix *How Do I Do That Again?*

Exercise 1: Creating a Collage

In this exercise you will be creating a collage.

☞ Open *Picasa*. ❧[8]

☞ Place five photos in the Photo Tray. ❧[22]

☞ Create a collage of these photos. ❧[49]

☞ Select the *Grid* layout. ❧[50]

☞ Select the *Mosaic* layout. ❧[50]

☞ Shuffle the pictures. ❧[51]

☞ Move the pictures and drag them to a different position by hand. ❧[52]

☞ Adjust the grid spacing so the border between the photos becomes broader. ❧[53]

☞ Set a solid color for the border (background) between the photos. ❧[54]

☞ Create the collage. ❧[55]

☞ Go back to the *Library*. ❧[20]

☞ Empty the Photo Tray. ❧[46]

☞ Close *Picasa*. ❧[4]

4.15 Background Information

Dictionary

Collage	A collection of photos that can be arranged on a page in various creative ways.
Gift CD/DVD	A slideshow on a CD or a DVD that can be played on a computer or a television set with a compatible DVD player connected to it.
Google+	A social network site by *Google*.
Google account	A combination of an email address and a password that gives you access to various free web services developed by *Google*.
Screensaver	A setting that allows the image on your screen to change at regular intervals if the computer is not used for a while. Originally, screensavers were developed to prevent screen burn-in by images that remain fixed on the screen for too long, but nowadays most screens are protected from these failures.
Slideshow	A collection of photos and video clips in a single folder or album, that can be viewed one after the other. You can set the slide's duration time as well as the type of transition to be used between the slides.
Title slide	A slide that contains text and that is usually the first slide in a slideshow, or that is used to mark a transition between various scenes. A photo can also be used as (background for) a title slide.
Transition	The way in which two consecutive slides flow into one another. Special animated effects are often used for such transitions.

- Continue on the next page -

Upload   Copy a file from your computer to the Internet, or to another computer.

Video   A collection of photos, video clips and sometimes music files that have been merged into a single file. While you create the video you can set the duration per slide and the style of the transition between the slides.

Video clip   A file that contains moving images and can also contain music tracks. Video clips are usually made with a video camera, cell (mobile) phone or webcam or downloaded from the Internet.

YouTube   A popular, free website for viewing video clips. If you register, you can upload your own video clips for others to view.

Source: Picasa Help

4.16 Tips

Tip

Background music for a slideshow

It can be even more enjoyable to watch a slideshow when it is accompanied by background music. You can use MP3 music files for this purpose. You first need to associate the folder that contains the MP3 files with the slideshow.

Click Tools

Click Options...

Click the Slideshow tab

Check the box ✓ by Play music tracks du

Click Browse...

☞ Select the folder with the MP3 files

Click OK

Now all the MP3 files in the folder will be played one after the other during the slideshow.

💡 Tip

Take a snapshot of a video clip

While you are playing a video clip you can take a snapshot of a single image:

To copy the image:

👉 **Click**

> Take Snapshot

The image will be copied.

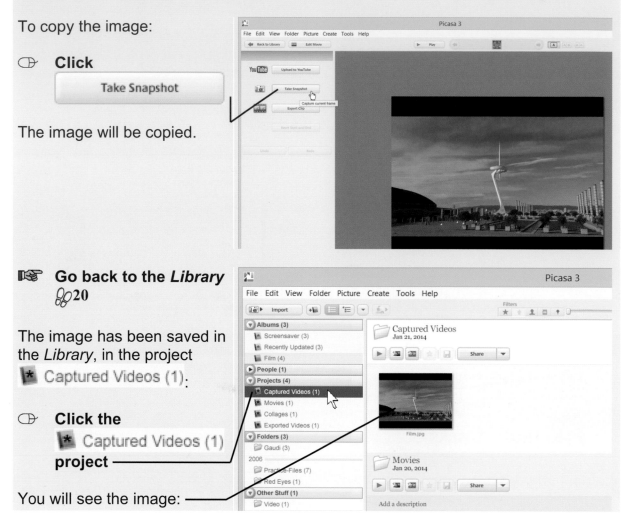

👉 **Go back to the *Library*** 𝒫20

The image has been saved in the *Library*, in the project ⭐ Captured Videos (1):

👉 **Click the** ⭐ Captured Videos (1) **project** ─────

You will see the image: ─────

💡 Tip

Shoot a video with the webcam

If you have a webcam you can place the images of this webcam directly into *Picasa*. Here is how you do that:

👉 **Click** 📹▶

The webcam images are saved in the ⭐ Captured Videos project.

💡 Tip

Delete a Google+ account
When your *YouTube* account was linked to your *Google* account, a mandatory *Google+* account was also created with its own profile. If you do not intend to make use of this social network you can delete the *Google+* account. This will prevent you from unintentionally publishing photos or videos online. If you delete the *Google+* account you will still be able to use other services by *Google*, but any videos that were uploaded to your *YouTube* channel will be removed.

☞ **Open *Internet Explorer*** 👣**1**

☞ **Open the plus.google.com website** 👣**2**

You may still be signed in. If you are not:

☞ **Sign in with your *Google* account** 👣**56**

Select your Google+ account:

👉 **By your email address, click** ▼

👉 **Click**

  Studio_Visual_Steps Google+ page

Open the page settings:

👉 **Click** ✦

👉 **Click** Page settings

👉 **Drag the scroll box downwards**

👉 **Click** Delete page

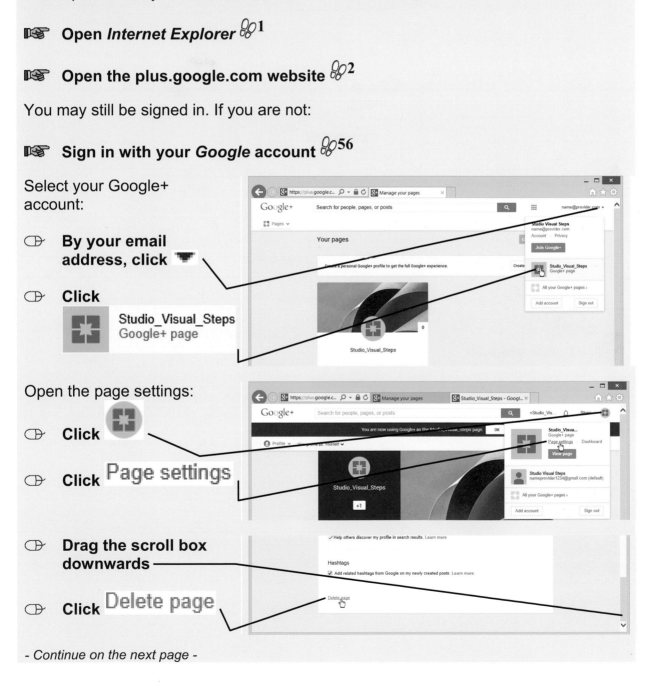

- Continue on the next page -

Please note: do not click **Delete page**. This option will delete your entire *Google* account and you will no longer be able to use any of the *Google* services.

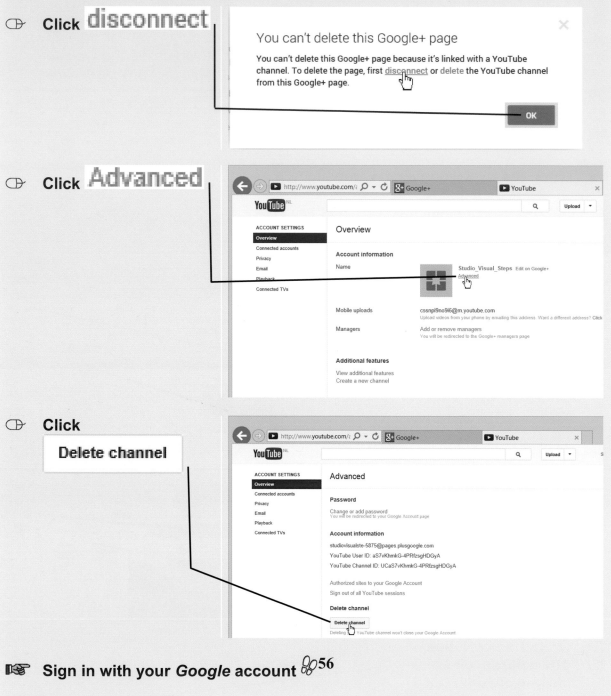

Click **disconnect**

You can't delete this Google+ page

You can't delete this Google+ page because it's linked with a YouTube channel. To delete the page, first disconnect or delete the YouTube channel from this Google+ page.

OK

Click **Advanced**

Click **Delete channel**

☞ **Sign in with your *Google* account** ⬿56

- Continue on the next page -

Click **Delete channel**

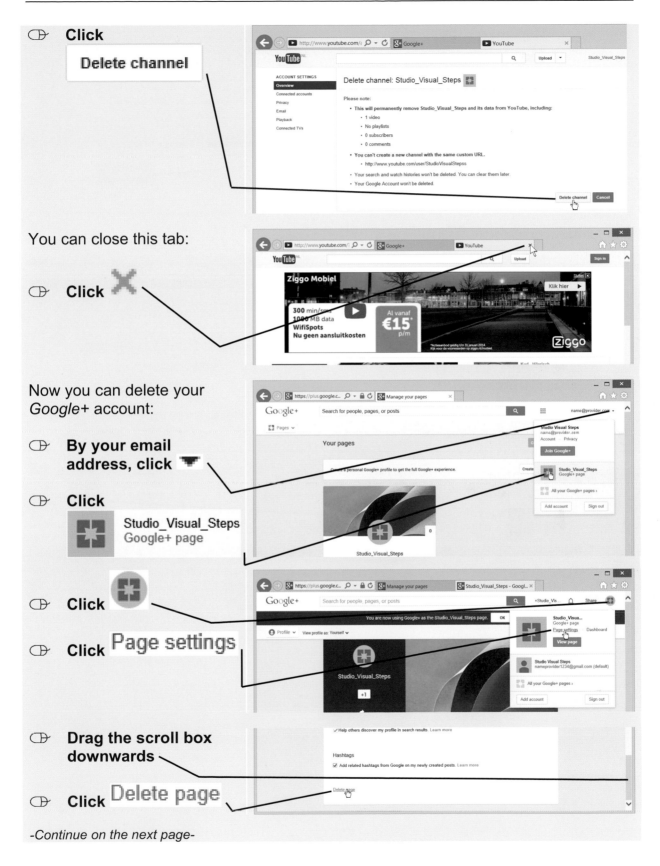

You can close this tab:

Click ✖

Now you can delete your *Google+* account:

By your email address, click ▼

Click Studio_Visual_Steps Google+ page

Click

Click Page settings

Drag the scroll box downwards

Click Delete page

-Continue on the next page-

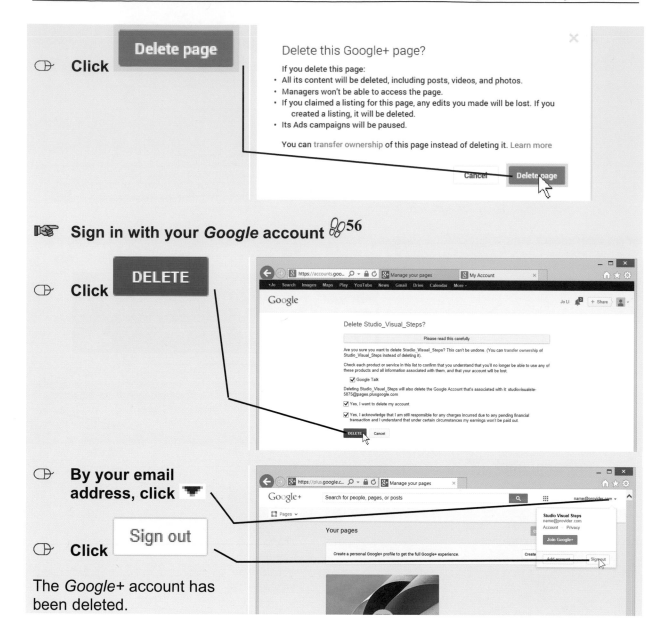

⊕ **Click** Delete page

☞ **Sign in with your *Google* account** ⅋56

⊕ **Click** DELETE

⊕ **By your email address, click** ▼

⊕ **Click** Sign out

The *Google+* account has been deleted.

5. Sharing Photos Online

There are several ways to share and distribute your photos digitally. You can share one or more photos in an email by adding them as an attachment to your message. In *Picasa* you can open an email message directly in your regular mail program and add the selected photo as an attachment.

If you want to share a larger number of pictures with others, a web album is much more convenient. You can invite people to view your web album online at their own convenience. They can then download the photos they would like to keep to their own computer. In this chapter you will learn how to create your own web album and synchronize this album with an album on your computer. In this way you can keep your web album up to date.

In this chapter you will learn how to:

- send photos by email;
- create a web album;
- upload photos to a web album;
- synchronize the web album;
- share your web album with others;
- upload photos with the *Drop Box* option.

Please note:

In order to perform the exercises in this chapter you need to have downloaded the *Practice-Files* folder and saved it to the (*My*) *Pictures* folder on your computer. In *Chapter 1 Setting up Picasa* you can read how to do this.

5.1 Sending Photos in an Email

Nowadays, photos are often distributed by digital means, instead of being printed and shown to friends. By email, for instance. You can send your photos directly from *Picasa*:

☞ **Open *Picasa* 𝒷𝒷⁸**

By default, *Picasa* will make the photos a lot smaller if you want to send them by email. In order to prevent this you can adjust a few settings:

⊕ **Click Tools**

⊕ **Click Options...**

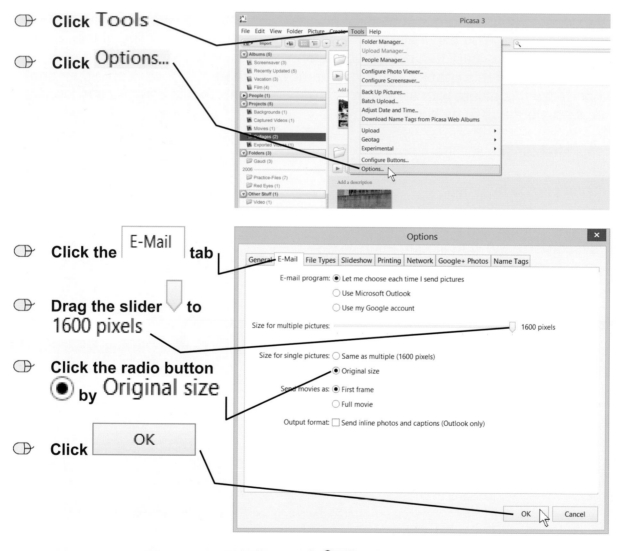

⊕ **Click the** E-Mail **tab**

⊕ **Drag the slider to 1600 pixels**

⊕ **Click the radio button ⦿ by Original size**

⊕ **Click OK**

☞ **Place two photos in the Photo Tray 𝒷𝒷²²**

At the bottom of the window:

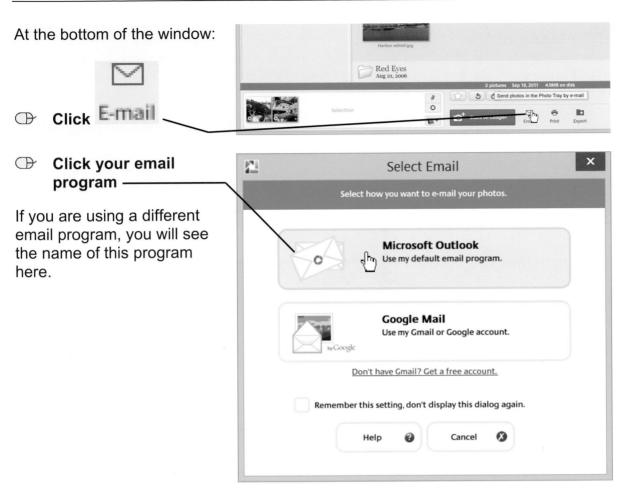

⊕ **Click** E-mail

⊕ **Click your email program**

If you are using a different email program, you will see the name of this program here.

You may see this window:

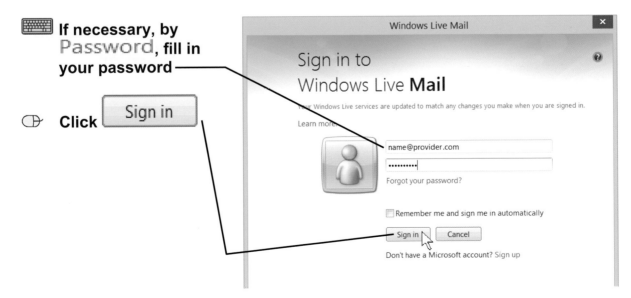

⌨ **If necessary, by** Password, **fill in your password**

⊕ **Click** Sign in

➥ Please note:

Unfortunately, if you are using the *Mail* app in *Windows 8.1* this option will not work. In that case you can send your photo as an attachment to an email message in the usual manner.

Your email program is opened and you will see the attached photo(s).

You can send the message in the usual way.

⊕ **Click**   **✕**

HELP! The email program does not open.

Does your email program not start, or do you get an error message? Then check the *Picasa* Help windows to read how to set up a default email program in *Windows*:

⊕ **Click** Help

⊕ **Click** Help Contents and Ind

Internet Explorer will be opened:

⊕ **Click** Share and manage a

⊕ **Click** Share via email

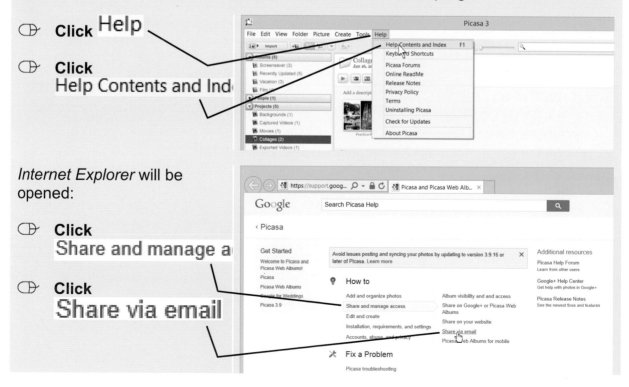

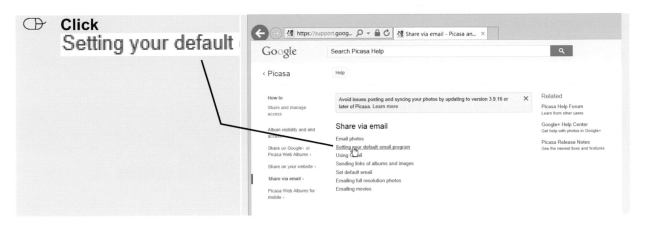

⊕ **Click**

Setting your default

☞ **Empty the Photo Tray** ᴼᴼ**46**

5.2 Picasa Web albums

A web album is a location on the Internet where you can place your photos and share them with others.

💡 **Tip**

Place the photos for your web album in a separate album
It is best to create a separate album for the photos that will be used in a web album. Then any modifications you make are saved to the web version automatically.

☞ **Create an album and call it** Vacation ᴼᴼ**11**

☞ **Add the photos named** *Salamander*, *Street* **and** *Tibidabo* **to the** *Vacation* **album** ᴼᴼ**12**

⊕ **Click** 🗀 Vacation (3)

You will see the photos appear in the album:

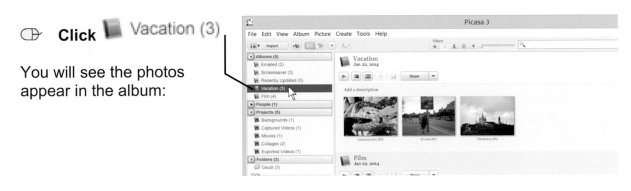

Add a short description:

👆 **Click**
Add a description

⌨️ **Type:** Various
vacation photos

⌨️ **Press** Enter

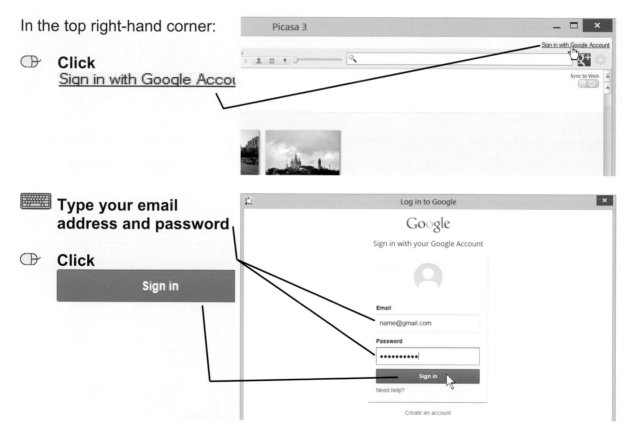

To upload the selected album as a web album, you need to sign in first to your *Google* account:

In the top right-hand corner:

👆 **Click**
Sign in with Google Accou

⌨️ **Type your email
address and password**

👆 **Click**
Sign in

If you do not yet have a *Google* account click Create an account. Then follow the instructions in the next few windows.

➥ Please note:

Google regularly updates the method for creating a web album. The instruction windows may also change, every once in a while. The windows we have used in this book may not correspond exactly to the windows you see on your own screen. Always read the instructions in the windows carefully.

You may see an *Accounts* window:

👆 **If necessary, click**

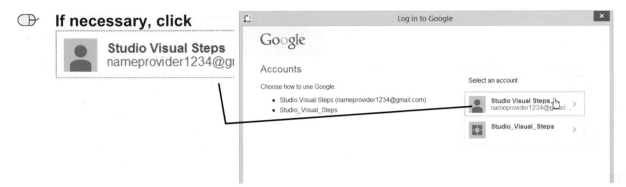

Now you can share your photos with others:

At the bottom of the window:

👆 **Click**

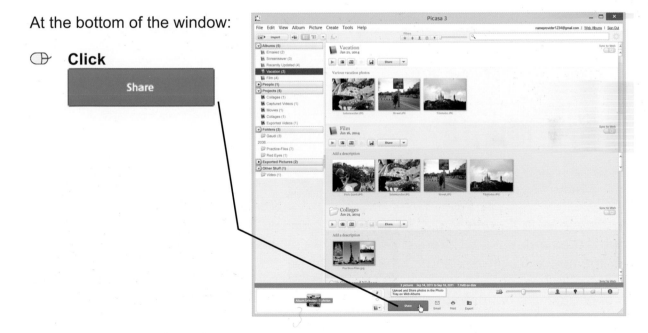

➥ Please note:

In this section, we are using a *Google* account that is no longer associated with *Google+* (see the tip *Delete a Google+ account* at the end of *Chapter 4 Fun and Useful Extras in Picasa*). If your account *is* associated with *Google+*, you will see some slightly different screens than the ones shown in the following sections. You will still be able to perform any action described.

You will see the *Upload to Web Album* window:

By default, the web album
has been given the same
name as the album in *Picasa*:

You can change the name for
this web album by clicking

| +🖼 New | and adding a
different name:

In this example, the web
album is only visible to the
people who will receive the
link from you:

In order to minimize the
upload time, the pictures will
be made smaller. But you can
select the original size, if you
prefer:

Add photos in their original size:

⊕ **By** Image size **, click**
▼

⊕ **Click** Original size

On *Picasa Web Albums* you
have a maximum of 1 GB free
storage space for photos and
videos. If you want to share a
lot of photos it is better to use
the smaller photo size. In the
Background Information at
the end of this chapter you
can read more about the free
storage space limits.

The people with whom you share the web album will receive an email message.

Here you can add a personal
message for your email, if
you wish:
For now this will not be
necessary. ———

To test how the mail will look
when received, you can add
your own email address:

☞ **Click**
    + Add people to
    share with...

⌨ **Type your email**
    address

⌨ **Press**

🔆 **Tip**

Suggestions
If you have saved any contacts in *Gmail* you may see some suggestions as you start
to type the email address. If you see the correct email address:

☞ **Click the desired email address**

You may also see some
suggestions for the groups to
which you can add as a
recipient. For now you do not
need to use these groups:

☞ **Click next to the email**
    address

If you want to allow the people who share this web album with you to be able to add their own photos to this album as well, you need to check the box ☑ by
Let these people contribute to my album .

Once you have entered the required information:

☞ **Click**

| Share |

> Email message
>
> [   ]
>
> [name@provider.com × |]
>
> ☐ Let these people contribute to my album
>
> Learn more...   Share 🖑   Cancel

🔖 **Please note:**

If you did not enter any email addresses in the *Upload to Web Album* window, you will now see the | Upload | button. As soon as the album is online you can still send emails with invitations to share this web album.

Here you see that the upload is in progress:

| 83% - Upload Manager — ☐ ✕ |
| Vacation   Cancel |
| Uploading - 3 of 3 (49% complete) |

When the uploading has finished:

☞ **Click** | View Online |

| Completed - Upload Manager — ☐ ✕ |
| Vacation   View Online |
| Finished: 3 items uploaded (message sent)   Clear |

You may need to sign in again:

☞ **If necessary, sign in with your *Google* account** 👣⁵⁶

You will see the web album on the *Picasa Web Albums* page:

📨 **Close the *Internet Explorer* window** 🐾⁴

You will see the *Picasa* window again:

🖰 **Click**

> **Clear Completed**

Completed - Upload Manager	— ☐ ✕
Vacation	View Online
Finished: 3 items uploaded (message sent)	Clear
☐ Conserve bandwidth	
Clear Completed 🖑	Hide

5.3 Synchronizing a Web Album

If you want to add new photos to your web album or replace photos you have edited, you will need to upload these photos again. By synchronizing your *Picasa* album with the web, the changes in this album will be transferred and applied automatically. First, you need to turn on the web synchronization option for the *Picasa* album:

In the photos that have been uploaded you will see the 🔼 icon in the bottom right-hand corner: —

🖰 **By Sync to Web, click**

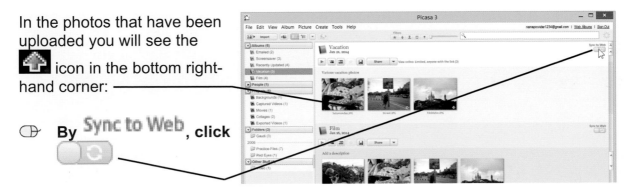

You will see the next window:

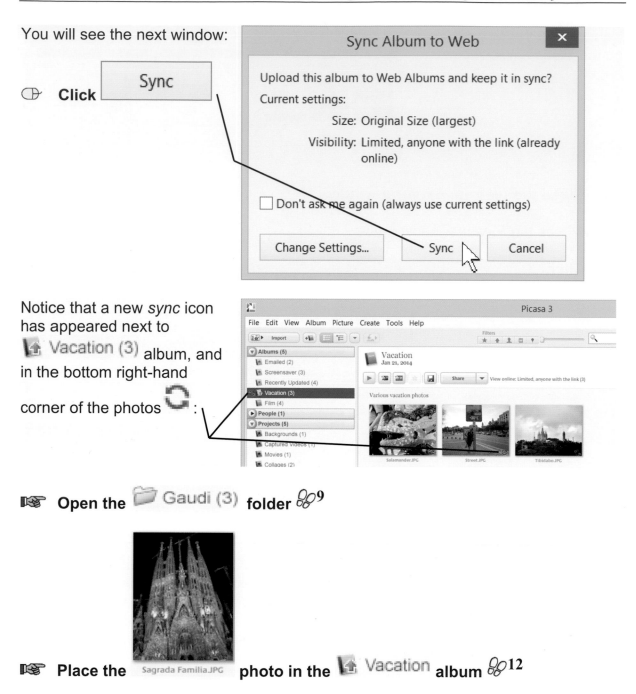

⏵ **Click** [Sync]

Sync Album to Web ✕

Upload this album to Web Albums and keep it in sync?
Current settings:

Size: Original Size (largest)

Visibility: Limited, anyone with the link (already online)

☐ Don't ask me again (always use current settings)

[Change Settings...] [Sync] [Cancel]

Notice that a new *sync* icon has appeared next to 🔼 Vacation (3) album, and in the bottom right-hand corner of the photos 🔄 :

☞ **Open the** 📁 Gaudi (3) **folder** 👣9

☞ **Place the** Sagrada Familia.JPG **photo in the** 🔼 Vacation **album** 👣12

➥ **Please note:**

If you have multiple photos in the album, the synchronization process may take a while.

Open the Vacation album 9

The photo you have added will be displayed in the album. Once the folder is synchronized, the icon appears in the bottom right-hand corner of the photo.

Click View online: Limited, anyone with the link (4)

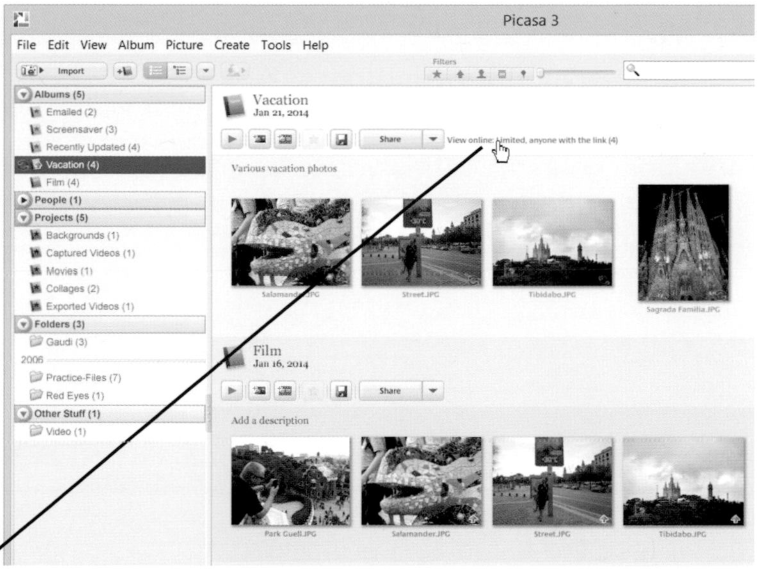

You may need to sign in again:

If necessary, sign in with your *Google* account 56

The new photo will also appear in your web album:

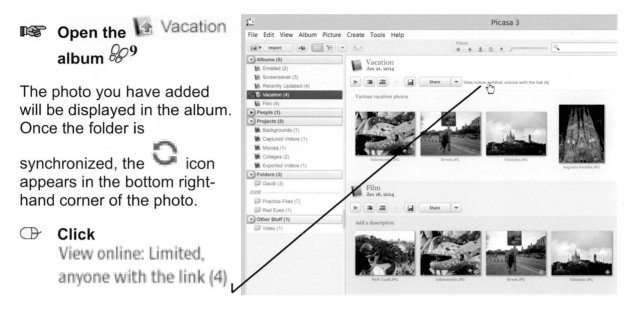

Click ×

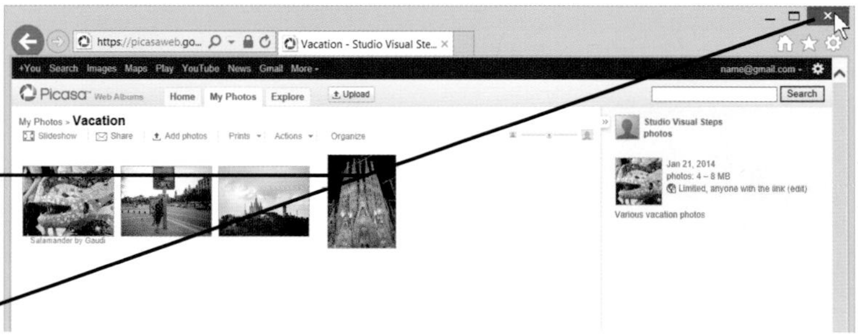

Tip

Turn off web synchronization

If you want to (temporarily) turn off the web synchronization option, for example, if you want to finish the album first, you need to click by Sync to Web: On. The photos that have already been uploaded will remain visible in the web album, but any changes you make will not be synchronized right away.

💡 Tip

Share a web album with others

With the `View online: Limited, anyone with the link (4)` link you can view your web album yourself. When you were creating your web album you sent an invitation to your own address. If you would like to invite others to view your web album, this is what you need to do:

👆 **Click** Share

You will see the same window you saw when you were creating your web album:

⌨ **Type your message**

⌨ **Type the email addresses**

Type a comma between the email addresses, when entering multiple addresses.

👆 **Click** Share

- Continue on the next page -

It appears as if the photos are uploaded once more, but that is not the case. The invitations are sent.

⊕ **Click**

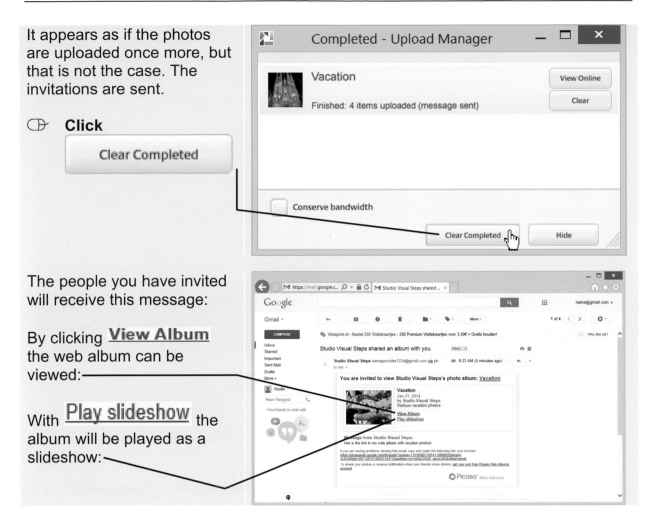

The people you have invited will receive this message:

By clicking **View Album** the web album can be viewed:————

With **Play slideshow** the album will be played as a slideshow:

5.4 Uploading Photos with the Drop Box

The *Drop Box* option is a fast method for uploading photos. It is a temporary web album to which you can upload photos from different folders, and then transfer them at once to the correct web album.

☞ **Open the** 📁 Practice-Files **folder** 🦶**9**

☞ **Open the** View.JPG **photo** 🦶**7**

Tip

Drop Box and Dropbox
You may be familiar with *Dropbox*, the free online storage service for files, images, and videos. The *Picasa Drop Box* option has nothing to do with the *Dropbox* service.

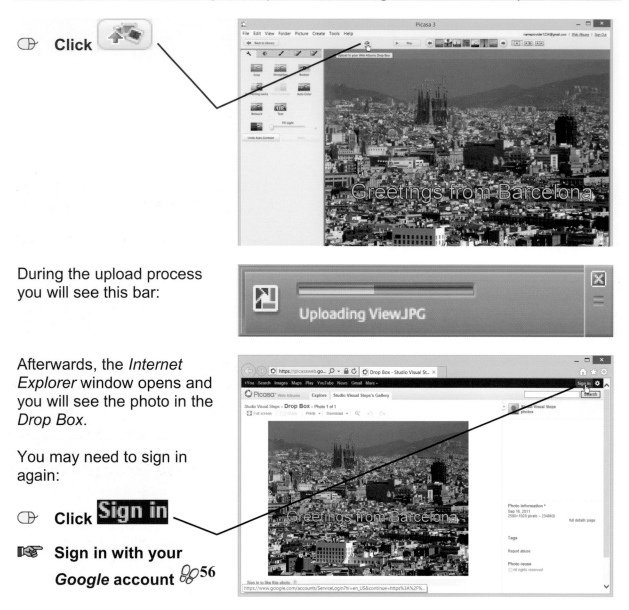

☞ **Click**

During the upload process you will see this bar:

Afterwards, the *Internet Explorer* window opens and you will see the photo in the *Drop Box*.

You may need to sign in again:

☞ **Click** Sign in

☞ **Sign in with your**
  Google account 𝒪𝒪56

Click

Now you will practice moving the photo to another album:

Click **Actions** ▼

Click **Move to another alb**

Click **OK**

Click **choose an existing alb**

⊕ **Click**

   Vacation
   Limited, anyone with th

At the bottom of the window:

⊕ **Click**

   Select Album

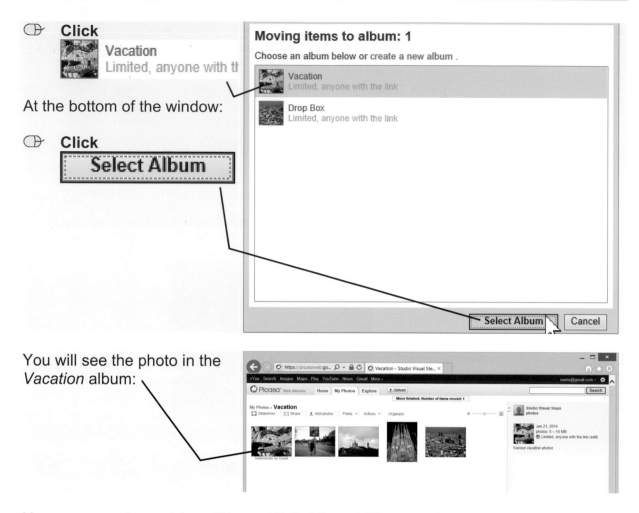

You will see the photo in the
Vacation album:

Now you can sign out from *Picasa Web Albums*. Then you can close the *Internet
Explorer* window:

⊕ **Click your user name**

   Sign out

⊕ **Click**

☞ **Close the *Internet Explorer* window** ⬮⬮4

You will see the *Picasa* window once again. Sign out from *Google*:

☞ **Click** __Sign Out__

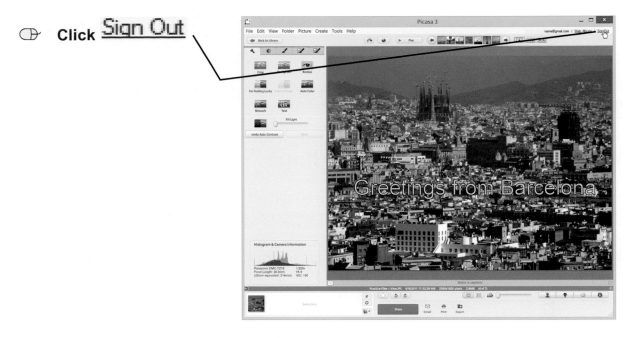

☞ **Go back to the *Library* ⚇²⁰**

☞ **Close *Picasa* ⚇⁴**

5.5 Exercises

The following exercises will help you master what you just learned. Have you forgotten how to do something? Use the number beside the footsteps *1* to look it up in the appendix *How Do I Do That Again?*

Exercise 1: Creating a Web Album

In this exercise you will be creating a new web album. We assume that you already have a *Google* account and that you have previously created a *Picasa* web album.

☞ Open *Picasa*. *8*

☞ Create an album and name it `Gaudi web album`. *11*

☞ Open the *Gaudi* folder. *9*

☞ Add the photos named *Sagrada Familia* and *Park Guell* to the *Gaudi web album*. *12*

☞ Open the *Gaudi web album*. *9*

☞ Add this description: `Art and architecture by Gaudi`. *57*

☞ Upload the album called *Gaudi web album* to *Picasa Web Albums*. *58*

☞ Clear the completed uploads. *59*

☞ Open the web album in *Picasa*. *60*

☞ Close *Internet Explorer*. *4*

☞ Sign out from your *Google* account. *61*

☞ Close *Picasa*. *4*

5.6 Background Information

Dictionary

Drop Box	A temporary web album that you can use to upload photos from various folders, after which you can transfer these photos to the correct web album.
Gmail	A free email service by *Google*.
Synchronize	To equalize; the content of the web album will be made equal to the content of the *Picasa* album with which it is synchronized.
Template	A template is the layout that determines how your blog messages are displayed.
Web album	A location on the Internet, where you can share your pictures with others. In *Picasa* you can use *Picasa Web Albums*.

Source: Picasa Help

Free storage limits

Picasa Web Albums offers 1 GB of free storage space for photos and videos. However, files under certain size limits don't count towards this free storage limit. This applies to uploads for other *Google* services that store photos and videos in *Picasa Web Albums*, including Google+.

If you have **not** signed up for *Google+*, the free storage limits are as follows:

- photos up to 800x800 pixels and
- videos up to fifteen minutes will not count towards your free storage.
- All photos uploaded over the free size limit will count towards your 1 GB of free storage. When you reach your storage limit, any new photos you upload to Picasa Web larger than the free size limit will automatically be resized to 800 pixels (on their longest edge).
- If you reach your storage limit while you are uploading photos with the *Picasa* desktop software you will only be able to upload at free storage sizes. Larger uploads will not be automatically resized to the free storage limit.

If you **have** signed up for *Google+*, these are the free storage limits:

- photos up to 2048x2048 pixels and
- videos up to fifteen minutes will not count towards your free storage.
- All photos uploaded in *Google+* will automatically be resized to 2048 pixels (on their longest edge) and will not count towards your free storage quota.
- All photos uploaded from the *Picasa* software or in *Picasa Web Albums* over the free size limit will count towards your 1 GB of free storage.
- When you reach your storage limit, any new photos you upload larger than the free size limit will automatically be resized to 2048 pixels (on their longest edge).

If you need more storage space you can purchase it. Monthly plans are available. For more information, visit https://www.google.com/settings/storage/summary

Source: Picasa Help

6. Printing Photos

From time to time you will surely want to show your pictures to other people. With *Picasa* you can print your photos or collages of photos yourself. It is very easy to select the right size and layout for the printed photos.

You can also let *Picasa* print a photo in the size of a poster. You can choose a percentage for enlarging the photo. *Picasa* will then proceed and divide the poster into a number of separate prints, each of 4 x 6 inches (10 x 15 cm) or 8 x 10 inches (20 x 25 cm), which you can glue together.

If you want to print a lot of photos it is easier to order your prints from a photo printing service, such as the Walmart printing service. This will cost you a bit more, but the photos will be printed in a higher quality, on special photo paper. The result is usually much better than if you print your photos with your own regular printer. In this chapter you will learn how to do this.

In this chapter you will learn how to:

- print photos;
- adjust print sizes;
- print a photo as a poster;
- order photos with a photo printing service.

➥ Please note:

In order to perform the exercises in this chapter you need to have downloaded the *Practice-Files* folder and saved it to the (*My*) *Pictures* folder on your computer. In *Chapter 1 Setting up Picasa* you can read how to do this.

6.1 Printing

You can print one or more photos in different sizes and layouts. First, you need to place the photos you want to print in the Photo Tray:

☞ **Open** *Picasa* 🐾⁸

☞ **Open the** 📁 Gaudi (3) **folder** 🐾⁹

☞ **Place the** [photo] **and** [photo] **photos in the Photo Tray** 🐾22

At the bottom of the window:

⊕ **Click** 🖨 **Print**

You will see various layouts for printing your pictures:

By default, the **Full Page** layout has been selected:

⊕ **Click** **5 x 7**

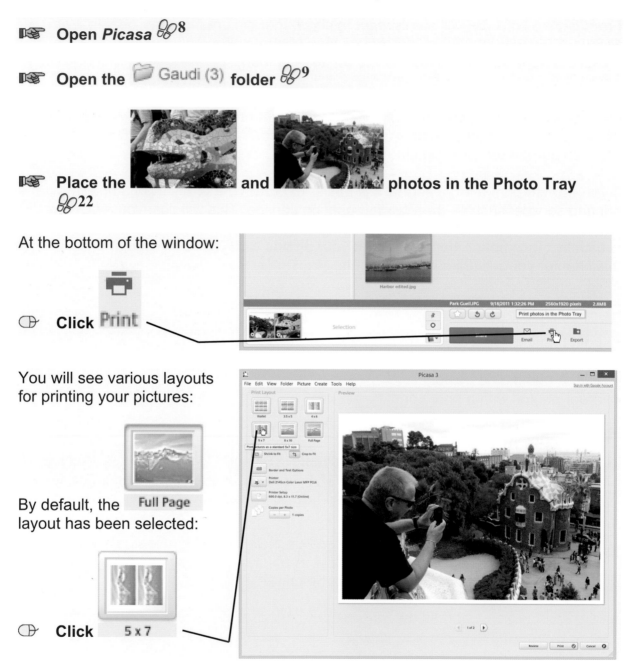

You will see a preview of both the photos in the Photo Tray.

🔖 Please note:

If you want to print a photo on a full page you will need to use a photo with a high resolution. Photos with a high resolution contain more pixels (image dots) than lower resolution photos. You may be able to adjust the resolution on your digital photo camera but this will depend on the amount of features available. A lower resolution photo will be less sharp if you print it on a full page and you may even see the individual dots that make up the picture.

If this is the first time you are printing, you need to select your printer:

☞ **By** `Printer`**, click**

☞ **Click the desired**
  printer

The photos in the preview
pane may shift a little.

When fitting the photo to the photo paper you can choose between two methods:

- `Shrink to Fit`: *Picasa* will shrink the photo both horizontally and vertically while maintaining the aspect ratio, so it will fit inside the selected size. Because of this, a white edge may be displayed all around the photo.

- `Crop to Fit`: The photo will be cropped (or enlarged) in a single direction, until it fits the selected size. The part that sticks out on the other side will be cut off. A small border of the photo will not be printed.

These options are important, because digital photos have a different height/width ratio, compared to the print size you selected. You can read more about this topic in the *Background Information* at the end of this chapter.

☞ **Click** `Shrink to Fit` **and** `Crop to Fit` **to see the difference**

💡 Tip

Change printer settings

If you want to print the photos horizontally (landscape orientation) you can change the settings:

⊕ By `Printer Setup`, click

The settings window of your printer appears. In this window you can select the orientation and the print quality.

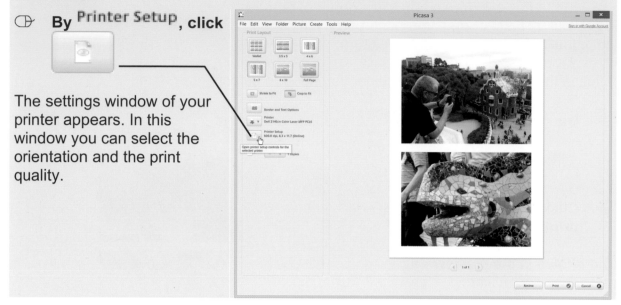

💡 Tip

Multiple prints per photo

Do you want to have multiple prints of each photo?

⊕ By `Copies per Photo`,

click ➕

The number of copies will be increased and you will see both prints of the first photo in the preview pane:

To view the next page:

⊕ Click ▶

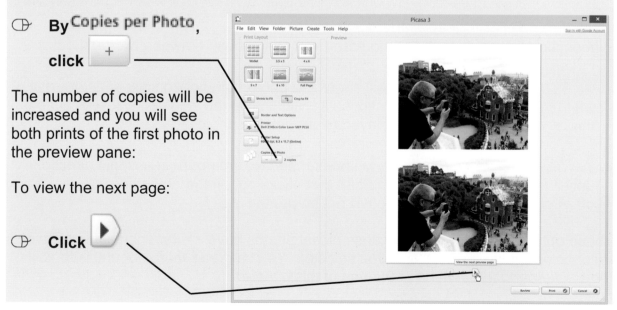

If you want to print the
photos:

⊕   **Click** Print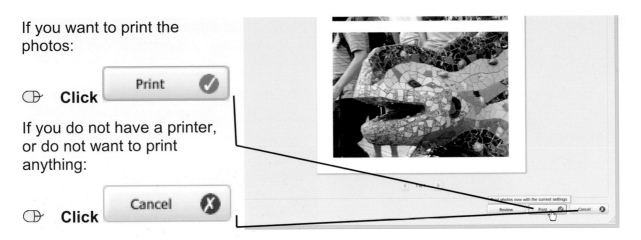

If you do not have a printer,
or do not want to print
anything:

⊕   **Click** Cancel

➥ **Please note:**

It is also possible to print photos directly in *File Explorer*. But if you want to print a
photo that you edited in *Picasa*, you will need to save the photo in *Picasa* first with
the *Save* or *Save as* options. Otherwise the original, unedited photo will be printed.

More information about saving photos can be found in *Chapter 3 Saving Photos*.

6.2 Making a Poster

With the *Make a Poster* function you can divide a photo into separate sections and
print each individual section. By joining these enlarged parts together again you can
make a poster of the original photo.

☞ **If necessary, open the** 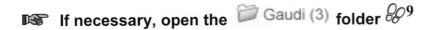 Gaudi (3) **folder** ℘℘[9]

☞ **Open the**  **photo** ℘℘[7]

➥ **Please note:**

If you want to print a photo as large as a poster you will need to use a photo with a
(very) high resolution. Photos with a high resolution contain more pixels (image dots)
than lower resolution photos. You may be able to adjust the resolution on your digital
photo camera but this will depend on the amount of features available. A lower
resolution photo will be less sharp if you print it on a full page and you may even see
the individual dots that make up the picture.

The *Make a Poster* function works best if the photo has the same size as the photo paper that is used for the print. In this example you will crop the photo to 8 x 10 inches (20 x 25 cm):

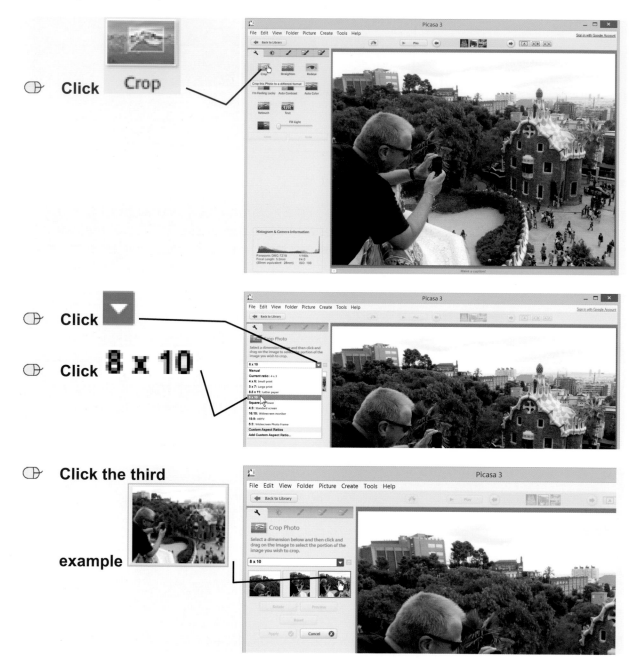

⊕ **Drag the frame to the bottom left-hand side**

⊕ **Click** Apply

Make the poster:

⊕ **Click** Create

⊕ **Click** Make a Poster...

You will be making the poster 4 times as big as the original photo. This means that the poster needs to be printed on 4 x 4 = 16 pages:

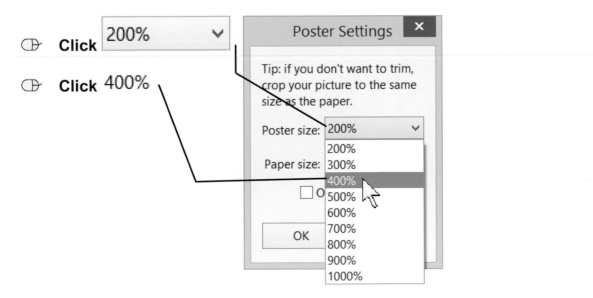

⊕ **Click** 200%

⊕ **Click** 400%

Use 8.5 x 11 inches (20 x 25 cm) paper size, which is the same size as the cropped photo:

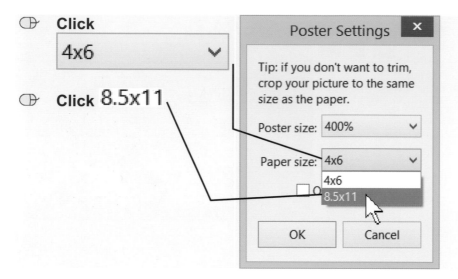

If you let the various pages (tiles) that make up the poster overlap each other a bit, it will be easier to join the pages later on. Of course, this will not be necessary if you intend to glue the pages onto some kind of background support.

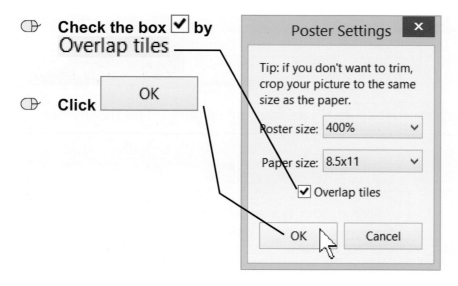

You will see a number of photos pass by in rapid succession. These are the individual photos that make up the poster. The last photo will remain frozen on the screen:

☞ **Click**

⬅ Back to Library

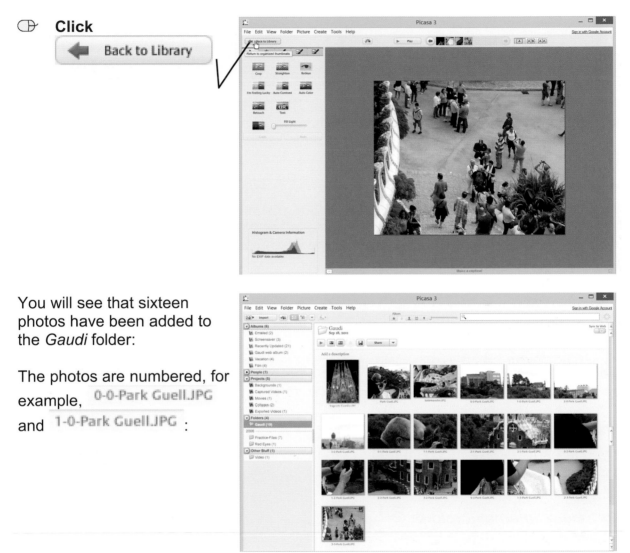

You will see that sixteen photos have been added to the *Gaudi* folder:

The photos are numbered, for example, 0-0-Park Guell.JPG and 1-0-Park Guell.JPG :

You can print these photos yourself, on A4 photo paper. Since the A4 paper size does not correspond with the 8 x 8 inch (20 x 25 cm) photo size, it is easier to let a printing service print this type of poster. They will have the correct 8 x 8 inch (20 x 25 cm) paper size. In the next section you can read more about photo printing services.

You can delete the photos for the poster:

☞ **Delete the sixteen photos that make up the poster from the** 🗁 Gaudi (3) **folder** ✂️13

6.3 Ordering Photos

Instead of printing photos yourself, you may want to look into using one of the excellent printing services that are available. Printing this way comes at a price, but the photos are printed in a higher quality and special photo paper is used. Usually, the result is much better than you can achieve at home with your regular printer.

If you want to print edited photos in *Picasa* it is best to save the edited photos with the Save As... function (see *section 3.4 The Save As Function*). When you do this you can give the edited photos a new name.

Tip
New folder
In order to have a clear overview of the photos you want to print, it is recommended that you create a new folder and save the edited photos in that folder. This way, you will quickly see which folder you need to use when you are going to upload the photos. In *section 1.5 Photos and Folders in File Explorer* you can read how to create a new folder in *File Explorer*.

In this example we will show you how you can quickly upload your photos to the Walmart printing service.

Most photo printing services require you to create an account. This will make it easier for you to upload your photos to your own account.

Please note:
If you already have an account with Walmart's photo printing service, you can continue on page 242.

☞ **Open *Internet Explorer*** 🐾¹

☞ **Go to photos.walmart.com** 🐾²

Click Start Here

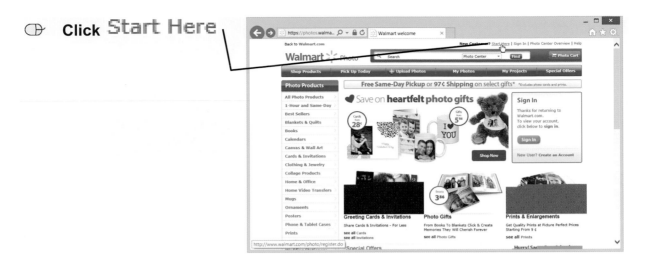

➥ Please note:

The Internet is continuously changing. Web pages are updated all the time. The Walmart website that appears on your screen may look a bit different from the images in this book. If that is the case, just look for a similar option or button.

Type the necessary information

Uncheck the box ☑ by Email Savings a

Check the box ☑ by Please check the bo Terms of Use.

Click **Register**

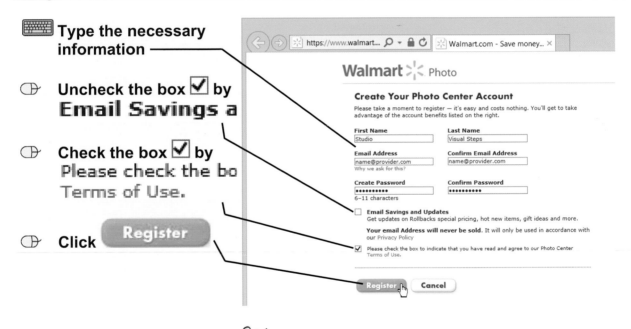

Close *Internet Explorer* 🦶🦶⁴

👆 **Click** File

👆 **Click**
Order Prints...

Picasa 3

File Edit View Folder Picture Create Tools Help

New Album...	Ctrl+N
Add Folder to Picasa...	
Add File to Picasa...	Ctrl+O
Import From...	Ctrl+M
Import from Picasa Web Albums...	
Open File(s) in an Editor	Ctrl+Shift+O
Move to New Folder...	
Rename...	F2
Save	Ctrl+S
Revert	
Save As...	
Save a Copy	
Export Picture to Folder...	Ctrl+Shift+S
Locate on Disk	Ctrl+Enter
Delete from Disk	Delete
Print...	Ctrl+P
E-Mail...	Ctrl+E
Order Prints...	
Exit	

Filters
★ ⚊ 👤 ▢ ⚑

Share ▾

Park Guell.JPG   Salamander.JPG

Share ▾

👆 **Click**

Choose

Shop   — ▢ ✕

◎ **Picasa**™   Back to Picasa

Prints & Products

Location: Walmart ⋇   4x6 prints starting at just 9¢. You can order online and pick up your
                                 Photo   prints at your local Wal-Mart photo center in one hour or have them
United States   ▾   mailed to your home. We also offer over 100 gift items, including
                                 Choose   photo books, mugs, calendars and more. Learn more...
Choose a Provider
                                 📷 **Life**pics   Print to any local camera, grocery, or drug store that uses LifePics,
You can order prints and   network   including CVS, Office Depot, Meijer, Albertson's, Hy-Vee, Ritz, Wolf,
personalized products from   Choose   MotoPhoto, Woodmans, & many others. GET $5 OFF YOUR FIRST
a variety of service   ORDER! Use promo code: LifePics05. Prints ready in 1 hour at
providers. Select a provider   many locations. Learn more...
from the list on the right,   shutterfly•*
and click the Choose   Turn the pictures you love into photo books, cards, prints and gifts.
button. Log into your   We'll never delete your photos and we offer 100% satisfaction

---

⌨ **By** Email**, type your**
email address

⌨ **By** Password**, type**
your password

⌨ **If you wish, you can**
type a new album title
by Album Name

👆 **Click** OK

Order Prints   ✕

Login

Photo Printer Site: Walmart

Enter the username and password you normally use to login to this photo printing
service. If you don't already have an account with this provider, click on "Create an
account" to sign up.

Email   Create an account...
Name@provider.com

Password   Forgot your password?
•••••••••

☑ Save Password   Login secured by SSL 🔒

Picture Size

To ensure the best quality prints, your images will be sent using the highest resolution
available.

Album Name
Gaudi

OK   Cancel

The photos will be uploaded to the Walmart Photo Organizer:

You can take a tour of the Photo Organizer. For now you do not need to do this:

☞ **Click** Close

The photos have been uploaded and placed in your online Walmart album.

You still need to select the photos you want to print:

☞ **Click the box ☑ by the photos you want to order**

☞ **Click** ⛟ **Order Prints**

☞ **Click** Prints

The photos will be placed in the *Photo Cart*:

☞ **Click** 🛒 **Photo Cart (2)**

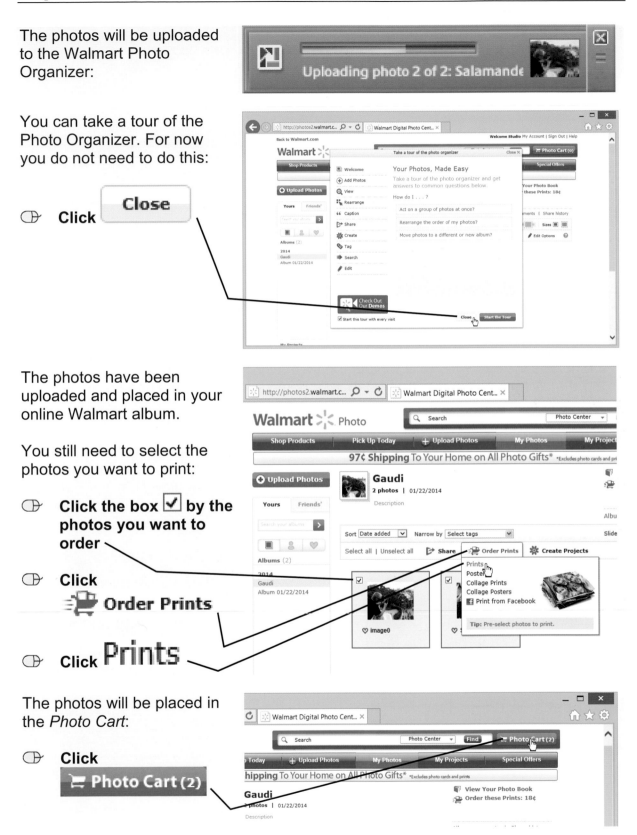

☞ **Select any other options, such as the photo finish.**

👆 **Click**

Proceed to Checkout

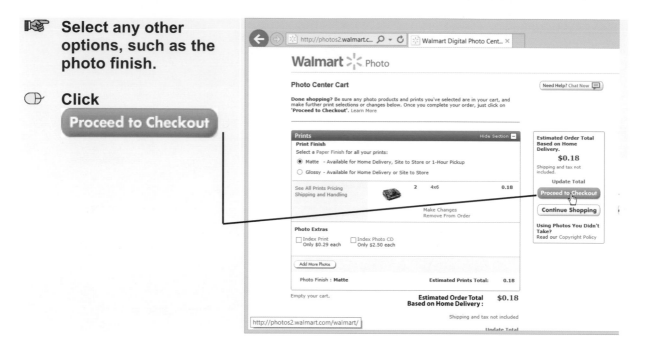

In the next few steps you will complete the payment process. The prints that are ordered at Walmart can be delivered to your home address or you can choose the store location and pick them up yourself.

🢂 Please note:

Besides the costs per printed photo your may also have to pay an extra fee for the ordering process or an administrative fee. Most online photo printing services will have information about the ordering process and these extra costs on their website.

☞ **Follow the onscreen instructions**

💡 Tip

Information on the Walmart order process
While you are ordering photos with Walmart you can use the Walmart Photo Help pages to guide you through the process. More information is available at: photos.walmart.com/walmart/helpindex

☞ **Empty the Photo Tray** 👣⁴⁶

☞ **Close *Picasa*** 👣⁴

6.4 Exercises

The following exercises will help you master what you just learned. Have you forgotten how to do something? Use the number beside the footsteps 🐾[1] to look it up in the appendix *How Do I Do That Again?*

Exercise 1: Printing a Photo

In this exercise you will be using the print option in *Picasa* once more.

👉 Open *Picasa*. 🐾[8]

👉 Open the *Practice-Files* folder. 🐾[9]

👉 Place the photos called *Tibidabo* and *Columbus* in the Photo Tray. 🐾[22]

👉 Open the print option. 🐾[62]

👉 Select the 3.5 x 5 inch (9 x 13 cm) print size. 🐾[63]

👉 If necessary, select the correct printer. 🐾[64]

👉 Set the number of copies to two. 🐾[65]

👉 Cancel the print command. 🐾[66]

👉 Empty the Photo Tray. 🐾[46]

👉 Close *Picasa*. 🐾[4]

6.5 Background Information

Dictionary

Resolution   The sharpness of a photo. The resolution is determined by the number of pixels that make up the photo.

Source: Picasa Help

Photo print sizes and aspect ratios
Old-fashioned photos have a height-width ratio of 2:3 (or in vertical position 3:2). Well-known sizes are:
4 x 6 inch (10 x 15 cm)
5 x 7 inch (13 x 18 cm)
8 x 10 inch (20 x 25 cm)

But digital cameras often use different aspect ratios, such as 4:3. Here are a few examples of the print sizes in pixels:
640 x 480 pixels
768 x 512 pixels
1024 x 768 pixels
1280 x 1024 pixels

This means that not every digital photo can be fully printed on regular sized photo printing paper. Part of the photo may be cut off, or you may see a white border all around the photo. You could compare this effect to watching a widescreen movie on a standard sized television. You will see a black bar, unless the image is corrected.

If you use *Picasa* to crop the photo to the right size before printing it, you can see a preview of what the printed photo will look like.

You can also use the [Shrink to Fit] and [Crop to Fit] buttons if you decide to print the photos (see *section 6.1 Printing*).

7. Working on Your Own Photos

You can import your photos in *Picasa* directly from your digital camera. Most digital cameras can be connected to your computer through a special cable. In this chapter you will learn how to transfer your digital photos from your camera or from a device with a built-in camera to your computer.

If the photos are already stored on the computer, you can use *Picasa* to scan the folders that contain pictures. Just read *section 1.4 Folder Manager* again to remind you how this is done.

Finally, this chapter will offer you some tips on photography in general.

In this chapter you will learn how to:

- connect your camera to the computer;
- import photos to *Picasa*;
- use various tips for taking pictures.

Please note:

In order to work through this chapter you will need to have a digital photo camera or a device with a built-in camera. The camera should have a few photos saved on its memory card.

7.1 Connecting Your Photo Camera to Your Computer

If you want to import your photos to *Picasa* you will need to connect your camera to your computer:

☞ **Open *Picasa* ⦿⁸**

A USB connection is the most frequently used cable connection for a digital camera:

You can often connect mobile phones, tablets and external hard drives with a USB cable as well.

You can also transfer photos to your computer by using the memory card of your camera. Although you will need to have a card reader to do this.

Here you see a built-in card reader on the front of the computer:

Different types of cards will fit into this card reader.

☞ **Connect your digital camera or any other device with a built-in camera to your computer and turn on the device**

Or:

☞ **Insert the memory card into the card reader**

If the camera or the device with the built-in camera has never been connected to the computer before, *Windows* will now try to install the driver software for the camera. The driver takes care of the communication between the camera and the computer.

If the driver has already been included in the *Windows* operating system it will be installed automatically. After the driver has been successfully installed you will often see the *AutoPlay* message on your desktop.

☞ **If necessary, close the *AutoPlay* window ⦿⁴**

➤ **Please note:**

There are several ways of connecting digital cameras to a computer. Be sure to check your digital camera's manual to find out more about these methods.

When you connect and turn on your camera, *Windows* may recognize the device right away. The corresponding driver will automatically be installed.
If your camera is not recognized, you can use the *Windows Camera and Scanner Wizard*. This wizard will help you find and install drivers for older types of cameras that are not instantly recognized by *Windows*. See the *Tip* at the end of this chapter to read how this works.

7.2 Importing Photos

This is how you start importing photos into *Picasa*:

In the top left-hand corner of the window:

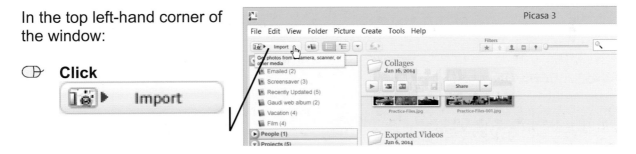

⊕ **Click**

If the camera or the memory card is not recognized at once, you need to select the device that contains the photos:

⊕ **If necessary, click ▼**
    by **Import from:**

Sometimes the brand and type of camera is displayed, but at other times only the memory card of the camera will be recognized. In that case your camera is called *Removable drive*.

⊕ **Click**
    Removable Drive(D:\)

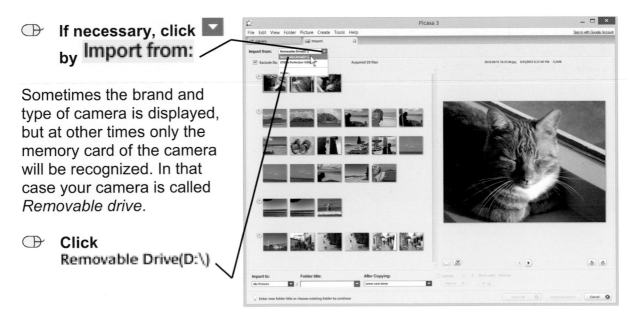

➥ **Please note:**

If you see this message **Copying 27 of 29 files at 128.6MB/sec** at the top, it does not mean that the photos are automatically copied to your computer. The program will download thumbnail images of the photos and you can view, select, and import these photos with the *Import* tab.

By default, the photos are imported to the *(My) Pictures* folder. This is how you create a new folder in the *(My) Pictures* folder:

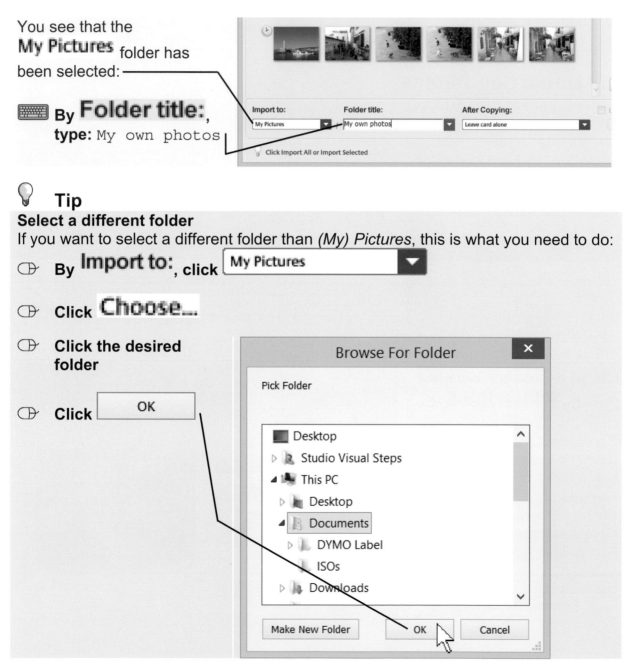

You see that the **My Pictures** folder has been selected:—————

⌨ By **Folder title:**, **type:** My own photos

💡 **Tip**

Select a different folder

If you want to select a different folder than *(My) Pictures*, this is what you need to do:

🖰 By **Import to:**, click **My Pictures** ▼

🖰 Click **Choose...**

🖰 **Click the desired folder**

🖰 **Click** OK

Now you will see the photos on your camera appear in the *Picasa* window:

If you want to import certain photos to your computer:

☞ **Click a photo**

Press Ctrl **and hold it down**

☞ **Click the other photos**

☞ **Click**

Import Selected (7)

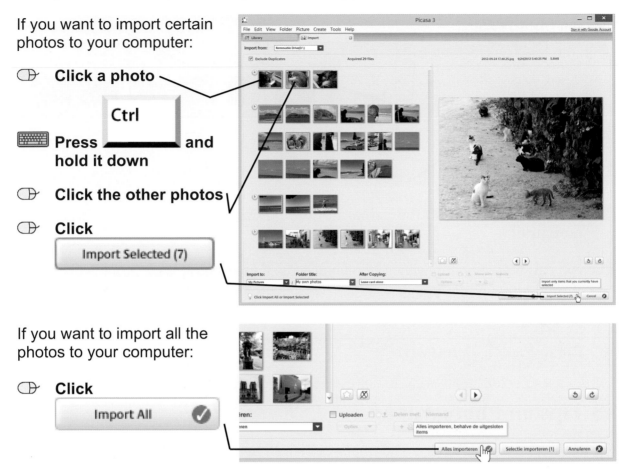

If you want to import all the photos to your computer:

☞ **Click**

Import All ✔

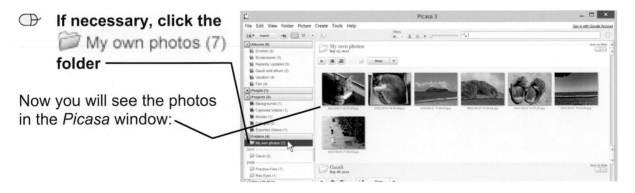

The photos will be imported and saved in the folder called *My own photos*, within the *(My) Pictures* folder:

☞ **If necessary, click the** 📁 My own photos (7) **folder**

Now you will see the photos in the *Picasa* window:

Take a look at the imported photos in *File Explorer*:

☞ **By** My own photos **, click** 📁

You will see that the photos have been saved in the My own photos folder, within the Pictures folder:

Close the window:

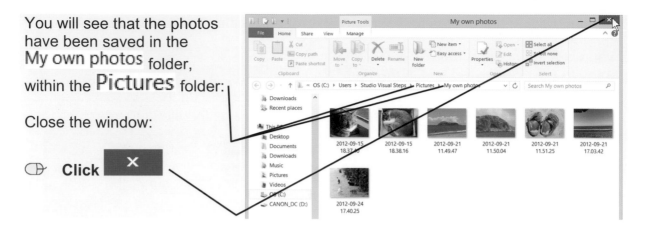

👆 **Click** ✖

☞ **If necessary, turn off the camera or the device and disconnect it from the computer**

Now you can start working with your own photos. If the photos have already been transferred to the computer you can let *Picasa* scan the folders that contain photos. In *section 1.4 Folder Manager* you can read how to do this.

☞ **Close *Picasa*, if you wish** 🦶⁴

7.3 Tips on Photography

You have almost reached the end of this book and by now you have learned quite a lot about editing photos in *Picasa*. You can use the tips below to take better pictures and enhance your own photos, so you will get better results when you edit them in *Picasa*. And perhaps you may not even need to use *Picasa* at all to edit them!

- Set the highest possible *resolution* on your camera. A picture that is taken with high resolution will contain a lot of pixels (image dots) and this means it will display a lot of detail. Editing and enlarging such a photo will produce better results.

- Try to keep the camera still while taking a picture, especially if you zoom in a lot on the subject. If you cannot use a tripod, then try to keep the camera steady by leaning against a wall, or putting the camera on the wall.

- Try standing a bit closer to the subject, or zoom in on it. This will place more focus on the subject and eliminate inconvenient items from the photo.

- Just take a picture of a detail instead of trying to capture the 'whole' picture; this can create a nice effect.

- Change your position. Walk around the subject, bend your knees, or stand a bit higher.

- Do not position the subject in the exact center; the photo will become more dynamic if you move the subject towards the edge of the picture. But make sure to control the automatic focus: first you need to focus by pointing the camera towards the subject and pressing the shutter release just half-way. Then you move the camera towards the final position and press the shutter all the way.

- By including a wall, the rail of a bridge, or a shrub in the foreground, the photo will acquire more depth.

- Keep the camera straight. Many cameras can display a grid on the LDC screen, which will help you keep the horizon straight while taking a picture.

- If you take pictures of a moving subject, then move along in the same direction and then take the picture.

- Use the natural light as much as possible. Using flash photography may spoil the mood of a photo. Many cameras have a standard setting for taking pictures without using the flash, such as *Night scenery, Night portrait, Candlelight* or *High sensitivity.*

- When using the flash you need to take the distance into account. If you are too far away the flash will not have any effect at all. And standing too close may lead to overexposure.

- Keep the sunlight behind or next to you. This will prevent annoying spots and reflections in the lens.

- A photo of a person or a group of persons in a static pose often gives an unnatural impression. Get the people to do something they enjoy, this works really well, especially with children.
- Do not forget to include the person's feet when you take somebody's full picture.

- In portrait photography you need to make sure that the eyes of the subject are just above the center of the photo, this will result in a nicer picture.

- By standing too close to your model you may distort the picture. It is better to keep your distance and zoom in.

- When taking pictures of people you need to make sure you have a quiet background, which will keep the focus on the model. But pay attention to the background; try to avoid giving the impression of a tree growing on top of someone's head, for example.

- Bright sunlight will often result in sharp shadows on someone's face. The softer light of a cloudy sky will produce better results.

- Use the Redeye correction when you take pictures of people while using the flash.

7.4 Visual Steps Website and Newsletter

By now we hope you have noticed that the Visual Steps method is an excellent method for quickly and efficiently learning more about computers, other devices and software applications. All books published by Visual Steps use this same method. In various series, we have published a large number of books on a wide variety of topics including *Windows*, *Mac OS X*, the iPad, iPhone, photo editing and many other topics.

On the **www.visualsteps.com** website you can click the Catalog page to find an overview of all the Visual Steps titles, including an extensive description. Each title gives you an extensive description and allows you to preview the full table of contents and a sample chapter in PDF format. In this way, you can quickly determine if a specific title will meet your expectations. All titles can be ordered online and are also available in bookstores in the USA, Canada, United Kingdom, Australia and New Zealand.
Furthermore, the website offers many extras, among other things:
- free computer guides and booklets (PDF files) covering all sorts of subjects;
- frequently asked questions and their answers;
- information on the free Computer Certificate that you can acquire at the certificate's website **www.ccforseniors.com**;
- a free email notification service: let's you know when a new book is published.

There is always more to learn. Visual Steps offers many other books on computer-related subjects. Each Visual Steps book has been written using the same step-by-step method with short, concise instructions and screenshots illustrating every step.

Visual Steps Newsletter
Would you like to be informed when a new Visual Steps title becomes available? Subscribe to the free Visual Steps newsletter (no strings attached) and you will receive this information in your inbox.

The Newsletter is sent approximately each month and includes information about
- the latest titles;
- supplemental information concerning titles previously released;
- new free computer booklets and guides;
- contests and questionnaires with which you can win prizes.
When you subscribe to our Newsletter you will have direct access to the free booklets on the **www.visualsteps.com/info_downloads** web page.

7.5 Tips

💡 Tip

The Scanner and Camera Wizard

In most cases the driver for your digital camera will be installed automatically. If your camera's driver is not automatically installed, you can try to install the driver software by using the *Camera and Scanner Wizard*.

☞ **Connect the device to the computer and turn it on**

This is how you open the *Wizard*. In *Windows 8.1* on the Start screen:

⌨ **Type:** scanner

⊕ **Click** View scanners and cameras

In *Windows 7* and *Vista*:

⊕ **Click** ⊞, Control Panel

⌨ **Type:** scanner

⊕ **Click** View scanners and cameras

⊕ **Click**

Add Device...

| Refresh | Add Device... | Scan Profiles | Properties |

Close

- Continue on the next page -

Now your screen may turn dark and you will need to give permission to continue.

☞ **Give permission to continue** ♐³

You will then see the next window:

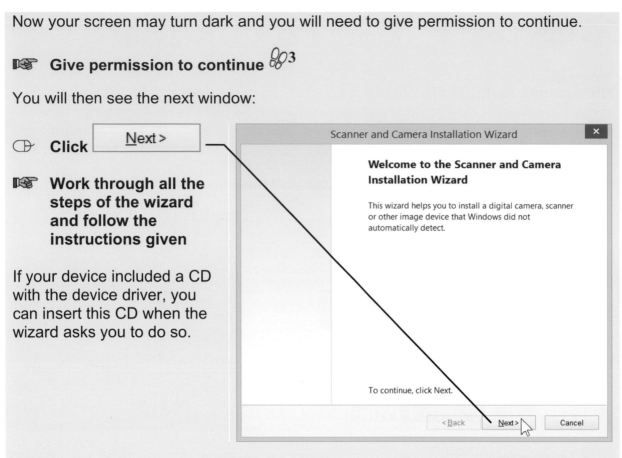

☞ Click [Next >]

☞ **Work through all the steps of the wizard and follow the instructions given**

If your device included a CD with the device driver, you can insert this CD when the wizard asks you to do so.

As soon as your camera is detected in *Windows* you will see the *AutoPlay* window.

☞ **If necessary, close the *AutoPlay* window** ♐⁴

Please note: sometimes you can also find information on the website of your camera manufacturer.

Appendix A. How Do I Do That Again?

The actions and exercises in this book are marked with footsteps: 👣1
If you have forgotten how to do something, you can read how to do it again by finding the corresponding number in the list below.

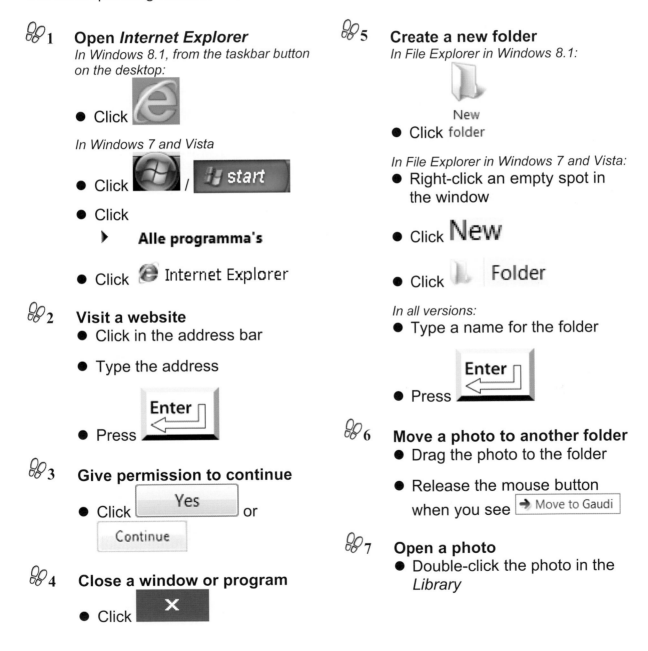

👣1 Open *Internet Explorer*
In Windows 8.1, from the taskbar button on the desktop:

● Click

In Windows 7 and Vista

● Click / start

● Click

▶ **Alle programma's**

● Click Internet Explorer

👣2 Visit a website
● Click in the address bar

● Type the address

● Press Enter

👣3 Give permission to continue
● Click Yes or
Continue

👣4 Close a window or program
● Click X

👣5 Create a new folder
In File Explorer in Windows 8.1:

New
● Click folder

In File Explorer in Windows 7 and Vista:
● Right-click an empty spot in the window

● Click New

● Click Folder

In all versions:
● Type a name for the folder

● Press Enter

👣6 Move a photo to another folder
● Drag the photo to the folder

● Release the mouse button
when you see → Move to Gaudi

👣7 Open a photo
● Double-click the photo in the *Library*

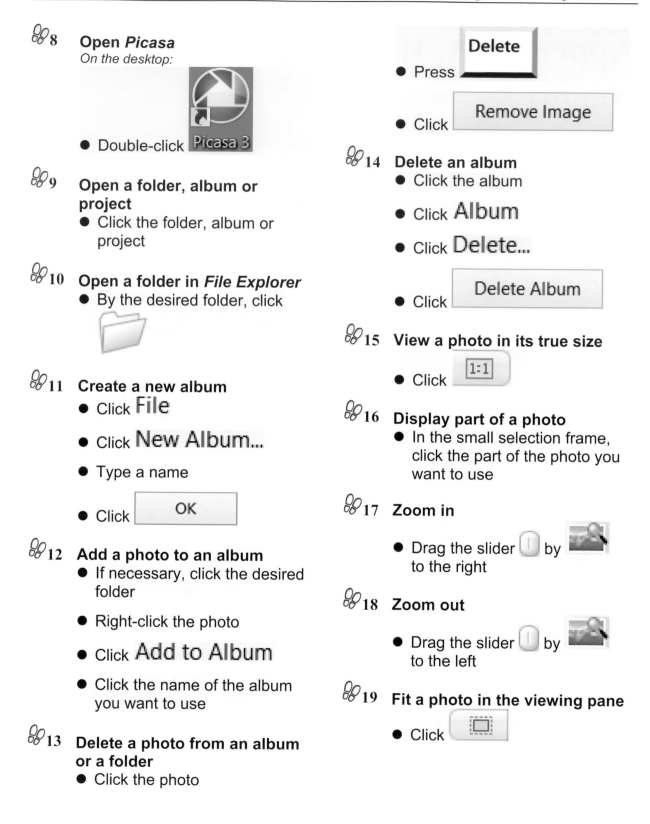

🐾8 **Open *Picasa***
On the desktop:

● Double-click Picasa 3

🐾9 **Open a folder, album or project**
● Click the folder, album or project

🐾10 **Open a folder in *File Explorer***
● By the desired folder, click

🐾11 **Create a new album**
● Click File

● Click New Album...

● Type a name

● Click OK

🐾12 **Add a photo to an album**
● If necessary, click the desired folder

● Right-click the photo

● Click Add to Album

● Click the name of the album you want to use

🐾13 **Delete a photo from an album or a folder**
● Click the photo

● Press Delete

● Click Remove Image

🐾14 **Delete an album**
● Click the album

● Click Album

● Click Delete...

● Click Delete Album

🐾15 **View a photo in its true size**
● Click 1:1

🐾16 **Display part of a photo**
● In the small selection frame, click the part of the photo you want to use

🐾17 **Zoom in**
● Drag the slider 🖱 by 🔍 to the right

🐾18 **Zoom out**
● Drag the slider 🖱 by 🔍 to the left

🐾19 **Fit a photo in the viewing pane**
● Click

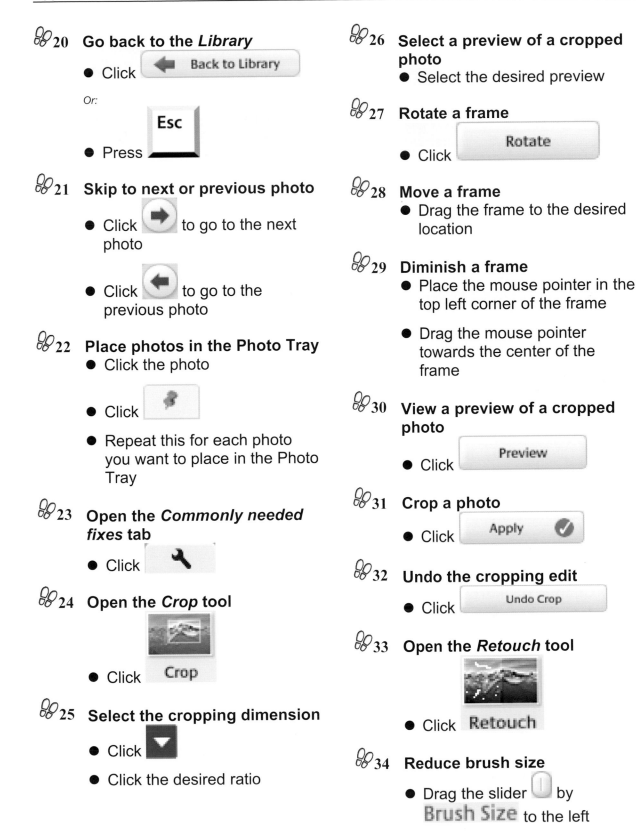

⧉20 Go back to the *Library*

● Click [← Back to Library]

Or:

● Press [Esc]

⧉21 Skip to next or previous photo

● Click [→] to go to the next photo

● Click [←] to go to the previous photo

⧉22 Place photos in the Photo Tray

● Click the photo

● Click [⚑]

● Repeat this for each photo you want to place in the Photo Tray

⧉23 Open the *Commonly needed fixes* tab

● Click [🔧]

⧉24 Open the *Crop* tool

● Click [Crop]

⧉25 Select the cropping dimension

● Click [▼]

● Click the desired ratio

⧉26 Select a preview of a cropped photo

● Select the desired preview

⧉27 Rotate a frame

● Click [Rotate]

⧉28 Move a frame

● Drag the frame to the desired location

⧉29 Diminish a frame

● Place the mouse pointer in the top left corner of the frame

● Drag the mouse pointer towards the center of the frame

⧉30 View a preview of a cropped photo

● Click [Preview]

⧉31 Crop a photo

● Click [Apply ✓]

⧉32 Undo the cropping edit

● Click [Undo Crop]

⧉33 Open the *Retouch* tool

● Click [Retouch]

⧉34 Reduce brush size

● Drag the slider [⬤] by Brush Size to the left

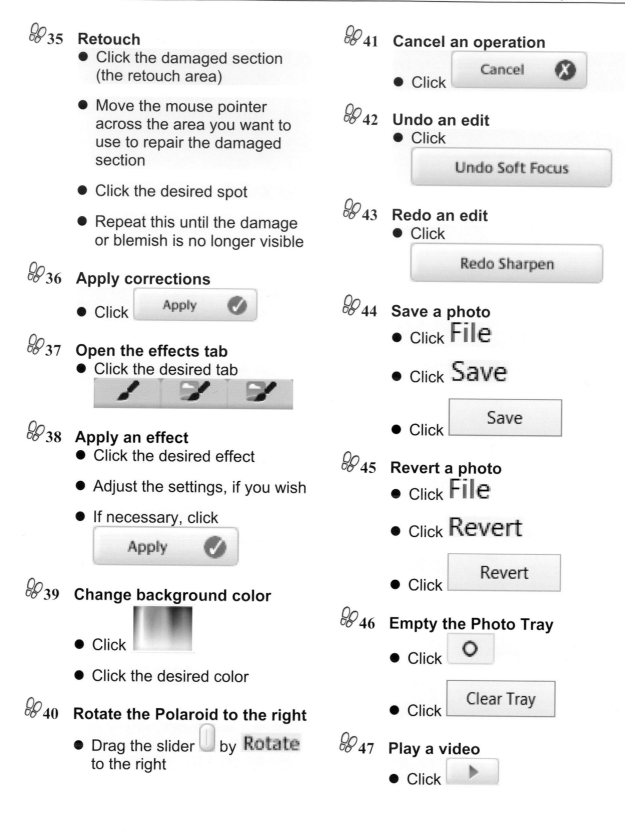

35 Retouch
- Click the damaged section (the retouch area)
- Move the mouse pointer across the area you want to use to repair the damaged section
- Click the desired spot
- Repeat this until the damage or blemish is no longer visible

36 Apply corrections
- Click Apply

37 Open the effects tab
- Click the desired tab

38 Apply an effect
- Click the desired effect
- Adjust the settings, if you wish
- If necessary, click Apply

39 Change background color
- Click
- Click the desired color

40 Rotate the Polaroid to the right
- Drag the slider by Rotate to the right

41 Cancel an operation
- Click Cancel

42 Undo an edit
- Click Undo Soft Focus

43 Redo an edit
- Click Redo Sharpen

44 Save a photo
- Click File
- Click Save
- Click Save

45 Revert a photo
- Click File
- Click Revert
- Click Revert

46 Empty the Photo Tray
- Click O
- Click Clear Tray

47 Play a video
- Click

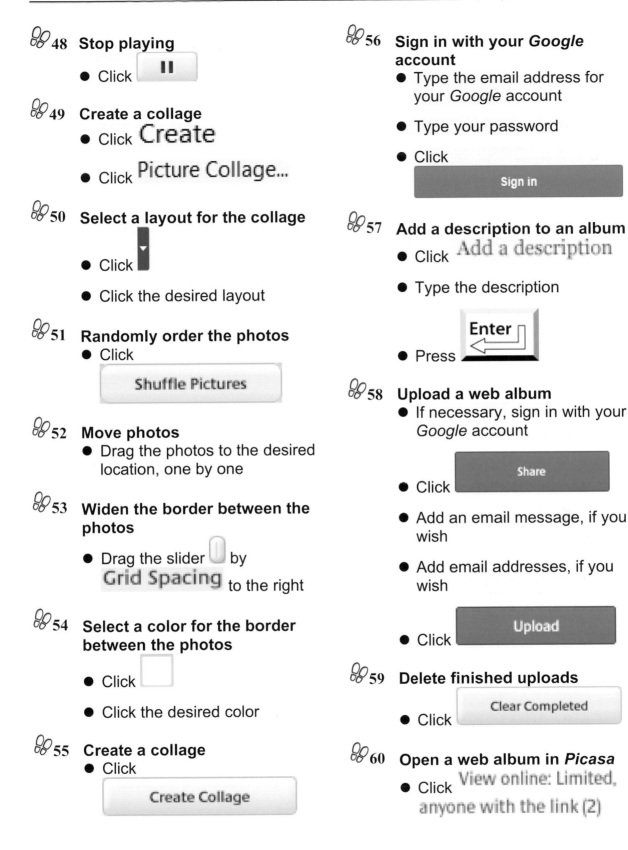

48 Stop playing

- Click ❚❚

49 Create a collage

- Click Create

- Click Picture Collage...

50 Select a layout for the collage

- Click ▼

- Click the desired layout

51 Randomly order the photos

- Click

  Shuffle Pictures

52 Move photos

- Drag the photos to the desired location, one by one

53 Widen the border between the photos

- Drag the slider by Grid Spacing to the right

54 Select a color for the border between the photos

- Click ☐

- Click the desired color

55 Create a collage

- Click

  Create Collage

56 Sign in with your *Google* account

- Type the email address for your *Google* account

- Type your password

- Click

  Sign in

57 Add a description to an album

- Click Add a description

- Type the description

- Press Enter

58 Upload a web album

- If necessary, sign in with your *Google* account

- Click Share

- Add an email message, if you wish

- Add email addresses, if you wish

- Click Upload

59 Delete finished uploads

- Click Clear Completed

60 Open a web album in *Picasa*

- Click View online: Limited, anyone with the link (2)

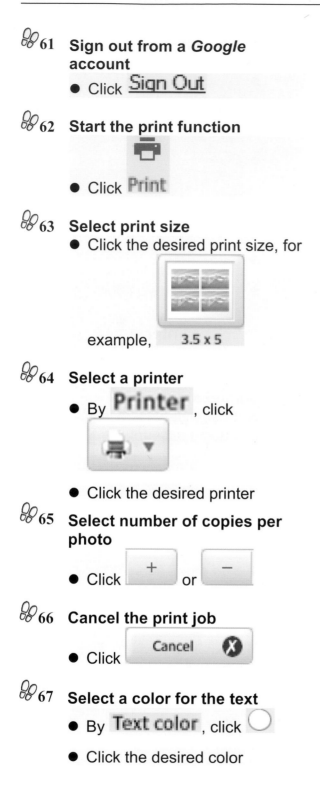

61 Sign out from a *Google* account

● Click Sign Out

62 Start the print function

● Click Print

63 Select print size

● Click the desired print size, for

example, 3.5 x 5

64 Select a printer

● By Printer , click

● Click the desired printer

65 Select number of copies per photo

● Click + or −

66 Cancel the print job

● Click Cancel ✖

67 Select a color for the text

● By Text color , click ◯

● Click the desired color

Appendix B. Removing Picasa

If you are experiencing problems with *Picasa*, you may be able to resolve them by removing *Picasa* from your computer first and then re-installing it. If you remove *Picasa*, the photos will still be stored on your computer and you can decide what to do with the photos you have already edited.

This is how you remove *Picasa*. In *Windows 8.1*, on the Start screen:

⌨️ **Type:** Picasa

🖱 **Right-click**

🖱 **Click** **Uninstall**

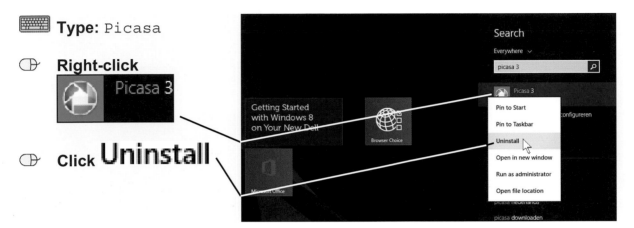

You will see the *Programs and features* window:

🖱 **If necessary, drag the scroll bar down**

🖱 **Click** ⚙ Picasa 3

🖱 **Click** Uninstall/Change

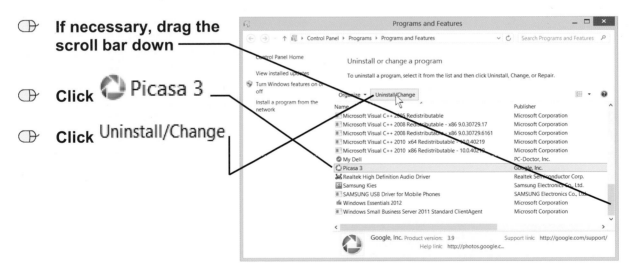

Continue on page 265, with the *Picasa 3 uninstall* window.

In *Windows 7* and *Vista*:

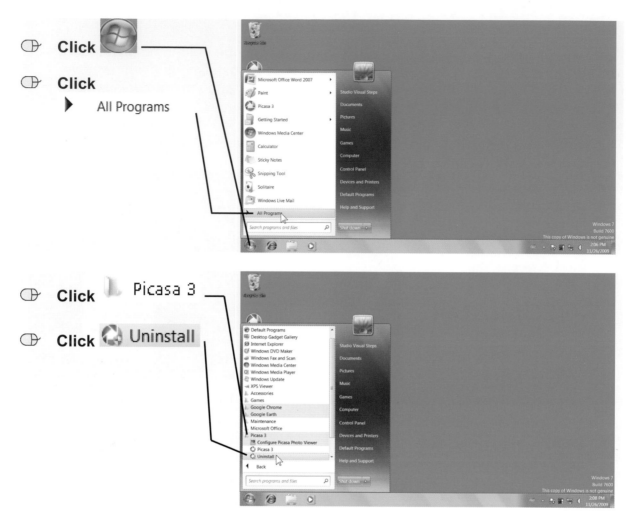

⊕ **Click**

⊕ **Click**

  ▶   All Programs

⊕ **Click**   Picasa 3

⊕ **Click**   Uninstall

If you are asked to confirm this operation:

⊕ **If necessary, click**  Yes **or** Continue

In all *Windows* versions you will now see this window:

👉 **Click**
[Uninstall]

Picasa 3 Uninstall — □ ✕

Uninstall Picasa 3
Remove Picasa 3 from your computer.

Picasa 3 will be uninstalled from the following folder. Click Uninstall to start the uninstallation.

Uninstalling from: C:\Program Files (x86)\Google\Picasa3\

Nullsoft Install System v2.42.4-Unicode

[Uninstall]   [Cancel]

Please note: first read the information below, before selecting an option.

👉 **Click** [No]
or [Yes]

Uninstall ✕

Would you like to remove the Picasa database?
If you are reinstalling click 'No'.

[Yes]   [No]

👉 **Please note:**

Select [Yes] if you want to permanently remove *Picasa*. All edits will be deleted along with your albums. The photos will be saved and you will be able to use them in other programs. If your photos are not displayed or positioned correctly in *Picasa*, it may be necessary to rebuild the *Picasa* database. In that case you need to remove *Picasa* too and click [Yes]. If you re-install *Picasa* afterwards, the files will be retrieved and placed in their correct locations.

If you select [No], the database with all the edits and the photos in their albums will be saved. Only select this option if you intend to re-install the *Picasa* program.

Internet Explorer is opened:

⌖ **Click** ✕

⌖ **Click**

    Finish

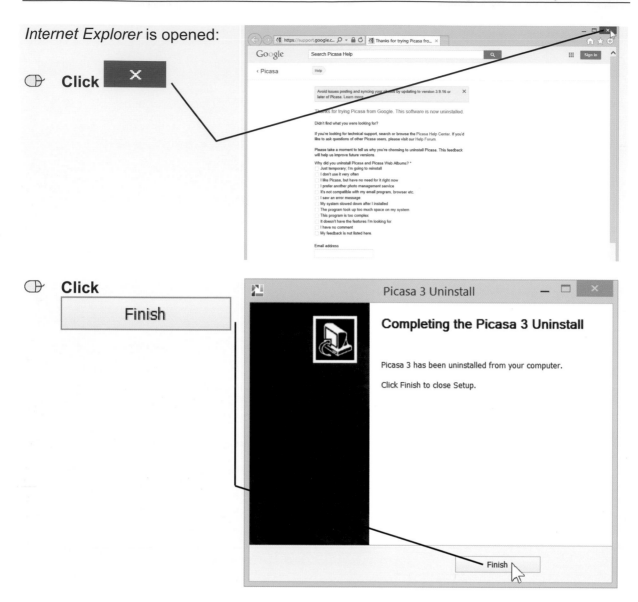

Appendix C. Index

Windows 8.1 for SENIORS

The computer book Windows 8.1 for SENIORS is a great computer book for senior citizens who want to get started using computers. The book walks you through the basics of the operating system Windows 8.1 in an easy step-by-step manner.

Use this learn-as-you-go book right alongside your computer as you perform the tasks laid out in each chapter. Learn how to use the computer and the mouse and write letters.

This book also teaches you how to surf the Internet and send and receive e-mails. Be amazed at how fast you will start having fun with your computer with the new skills and information you will gain!

GET STARTED QUICKLY WITH WINDOWS 8.1

Author: Studio Visual Steps
ISBN 978 90 5905 118 8
Book type: Paperback, full color
Nr of pages: 368 pages
Accompanying website: www.visualsteps.com/windows8

You will learn how to:
- become comfortable and enjoy using your computer
- write letters and memos on the computer
- send and receive messages by e-mail
- explore the World Wide Web
- customize your computer settings

Suitable for:
Windows 8.1 on a desktop or laptop computer

Samsung Galaxy Tab for SENIORS

The Samsung Galaxy Tab and the Note are extremely user friendly, portable multimedia devices that offer a wide range of possibilities. They are both suitable for many different purposes. For instance, sending and receiving email messages, surfing the Internet, taking notes, planning a trip, or keeping a calendar.

GET MORE OUT OF YOUR SAMSUNG GALAXY TAB

The Samsung Galaxy Tab and the Note come equipped with a large number of standard apps (programs) that you can use for instance, to work with photos, videos, and music. You can also immediately share your photos with others.

Apart from that, you can search the Play Store for many more free and paid apps. What about games, puzzles, newspapers, magazines, fitness exercises, and photo editing apps? You can find apps for almost any purpose you can think of.

In this book you will learn to use the main options and functions of this versatile tablet.

Author: Studio Visual Steps
ISBN 978 90 5905 089 1
Book type: Paperback, full color
Nr of pages: 264 pages
Accompanying website:
www.visualsteps.com/ samsungtab

Full color!

You will learn how to:
- operate the Samsung Galaxy Tab and Note
- connect to a Wi-Fi or mobile data network
- surf the Internet and use e-mail
- use built-in applications
- download apps from the App Store
- work with photos, video and music

Suitable for:
Samsung Galaxy Tab 2, 3, Note and Note 2014 edition.